GREAT CIVIL WAR STORIES OF KENTUCKY

Great Civil War Stories of Kentucky

Marshall Myers

Acclaim Press
MORLEY, MISSOURI

Acclaim Press
Your Next Great Book
P.O. Box 238
Morley, MO 63767
(573) 472-9800
www.acclaimpress.com

Book Design: Tiffany Glastetter
Cover Design: M. Frene Melton

Copyright © 2011 Marshall Myers

All Rights Reserved.

No part of this book shall be reproduced or transmitted in any form or by any means, electronic or mechanical, including photocopying, recording or by an information or retrieval system, except in the case of brief quotations embodied in articles and reviews, without the prior written consent of the publisher. The scanning, uploading and distribution of this book via the Internet or via any other means without permission of the publisher is illegal and punishable by law.

Library of Congress has cataloged the hardcover edition as follows:
  Myers, Marshall.
  Great Civil War Stories of Kentucky / by Marshall Myers.
    p. cm.
  Includes index.
  ISBN-13: 978-1-935001-72-0 (alk. paper)
  ISBN-10: 1-935001-72-8 (alk. paper)
  1. Kentucky--History--Civil War, 1861-1865. 2. Kentucky--History--Civil War, 1861-1865--Social aspects. 3. Kentucky--History--Civil War, 1861-1865--Biography.   I. Title.
  E509.M94 2011
  976.9'03--dc22

                       2011013404

First Paperback Edition, Printed 2021
ISBN: 978-1-956027-05-1 | 1-956027-05-X

Printed in the United States of America
10 9 8 7 6 5 4 3 2 1

Contents

Acknowledgments 9

Introduction 11

Lessons Lincoln Learned in Kentucky 17

Lincoln, the Law and a Lady
    A Kentucky Connection 27

Lincoln's Poetry
    A Look Inside 33

Abraham Lincoln and the Other Mary from Kentucky 37

Lincoln's Last Visits to Kentucky 45

What did Kentuckians Think of Lincoln? 49

Henry Clay's Influence on Lincoln
    The Lessons Lincoln Learned 57

Kentucky's Senator John S. Crittenden
    His Attempts to Prevent the Civil War 63

Confederate General Ben Hardin Helm
    A Promising Kentuckian Dies Too Young 71

Kentuckian Emilie Todd Helm
    "Little Sister" Causes a Stir at the White House 77

General Humphrey Marshall
    A Little Too Political to be Military 83

Englishman George St. Leger Grenfell
    General John Hunt Morgan's Military Man 89

"Lightning Ellsworth"
  Morgan's Telegraph Man 95

Madison County's James Bennett McCreary
  From Morgan's Soldier to U.S. Senator 99

**Confederate General Braxton Bragg and General
John Cabell Breckinridge**
  Feuding, Fighting and Fidgeting During the Civil War 113

**Confederate Captain Thomas Hines' Narrow Escape at
Blue River Island in Lower Meade County** 121

**Kentuckian Thomas Henry Hines and
The Northwest Conspiracy** 127

The Feeding of the Hordes
  The Civil War and the Shakers at Pleasant Hill 133

The War on the Home Front
  Lexington, Kentucky 139

Life for Kentuckians at Camp Douglas, a Civil War Prison 145

**Religion in the Civil War and the Good Parson
Wynne's Dilemma** 151

The Case of Dr. Mary Edwards Walker
  What Really Happened in That Louisville Civil War Prison? ... 157

Day to Day in the Orphan Brigade 163

Loreta Velazquez at Lt. Harry T. Buford, C.S.A.
  A Kentucky Connection 171

Blood and Smoke
  Kentuckian Major Walker Taylor's Plot to Abduct Lincoln 179

Kentucky's Corporal Andrew Jackson Smith
  Civil War Hero for his Country and for African Americans 185

Greensburg's General Edward Hobson
  An Ordinary Soldier Doing Extraordinary Things 193

Confederate General Hylan Benton Lyon
  Fighting Hard and Raising Cain 203

Kentucky's Confederate Trickster
  General Adam "Stovepipe" Johnson 211

About the Author 219

Index 220

Acknowledgments

No publication is the product of just one person's mind. And this work certainly does not depart from that maxim. In writing these articles over fourteen years, scholars and trained historians much more learned than I have offered tidbits of wisdom, critical but wise advice, and invaluable suggestions that guided me to places and people I would have never explored on my own. The faults in this work, however, are mine, not theirs.

A number of people warrant mentioning by name. They include Charles Hayes at *Kentucky Explorer*, and William Matthews and Jerlene Rose at Back Home in Kentucky, who published many of these articles in their fine magazines. Among countless others, I should name Charles Hay and the members of the Madison County Civil War Roundtable, who encouraged me to write these brief glimpses into our nation's most important war. Dr. James Klotter, State Historian, and Lowell Harrison, late of Western Kentucky University, often helped me to see what excellent historians do well by showing what this pair of historians does so well. Various staff and faculty of the Department of English at Eastern Kentucky University, who also gracefully endured my constant jabbering about the Civil War, deserve mentioning. My wife, Dr. Lynn Gillaspie, who understands my often-disjointed passion for the Civil War in Kentucky, has graciously tolerated my need to explore and to write about what I have found.

Most of all, I owe an eternal debt to my late mother, Carol Cushman Myers, and my father, Clarice Myers, Jr., who lit a fire in me, added kindling by helping me to appreciate the richness of Kentucky by buying me books, and taking me to important places in the Commonwealth, and finally added wood to the blaze by encouraging my writing. Perhaps these stories will repay in part my debt for what these Kentucky transplants from the rolling hills of southwestern Wisconsin did for me.

Dr. Marshall Myers
Richmond, Kentucky

Introduction

After fourteen years, reading and writing about the Civil War in Kentucky remain for me two fascinating pursuits for a number of reasons. For example, the dark days before the war actually began when politicians wooed Kentucky, North and South, testify to the independent spirit that characterizes many Kentuckians even today. Both sides wanted the Commonwealth for not only her agricultural riches or her political clout, but also because both sides recognized the geographic importance of that buffer of land between them and their enemies.

In many ways, Kentucky during this great conflict also truly mirrored more than any other state the idea of the Civil War as an internecine conflict, brother against brother, so much so that in many families in Kentucky, it was literally true, often with two brothers siding with different causes, even father and son splitting their family's allegiances.

While the Bluegrass and far western Kentucky were largely Confederate in their sympathies, and while the eastern mountains mostly aligned with the Union, still pockets of resistance within areas were quite common, lending a certain troubling ambiguity about just which side a particular county or city was on to those fighting the war.

Several important battles also took place in the Commonwealth, including engagements at Wildcat Mountain, Middle Creek, Mill Springs, Richmond, and the "Battle for Kentucky," a bloody affair at Perryville. While not all these engagements matched the bloodletting and havoc at Perryville and other places, the early Union victories at Mill Spring, Middle Creek, and Wildcat Mountain often were the only good news for the Union in those early frustrating years of the war. The Rebels won victory after victory in the East, and hopes for a quick Union victory seemed the figment of a fool's imagination.

The war soon became a guerrilla war in the state after the frustrating losses by the Confederacy, particularly at Perryville. Not surprisingly, then, some students of the war in Kentucky see General John Hunt Morgan and his Boys in Butternut as actually Rebels largely out of control under a Confederate general who seemed happier spreading panic than from actually capturing territory; they became merely a large band of uniformed guerrillas, if you will. Significantly, though, Morgan became the ultimate Confederate hero in the state after the war, a man who seemed to exude the Southern myth Kentucky style. But as charismatic as Morgan was, those who rode with him or trained under him wrote some fascinating chapters in Kentucky Civil War history, too.

Yet in the lives of most Kentuckians, the war meant senseless murders, and rampant destruction of property, crops, and livestock, carried out by roving bands of Confederates, often homegrown, who exacted revenge for Kentucky's remaining in the Union, or who felt that guerrilla warfare was the only effective way of winning the sympathies of a reluctant citizenry, who by that time had begun turning their eyes South. The sheer number of engagements between guerrillas and local "home guards" is staggering, with nearly every county in the state suffering some kind of guerrilla warfare. State Historian James Klotter calls it "the everyday experience" of Kentucky's citizenry.

Even though Kentuckians and scholars of the war have rightfully written much about the highlights of the conflict in the state, countless episodes and incidents, colorful characters, and even lighter moments have been largely overlooked, and need chronicling. In fact, in part, the subject of this book is to tell the untold tales that describe what the Civil War was like for many in the Commonwealth.

Often overlooked, though, are the significant contributions African Americans from Kentucky made. Only Louisiana, under strict Union military control, sent more "colored" troops (as they were called in those days) to the Union cause. Little is known about their war experiences, yet what is known about these valiant warriors affirms that their stories need telling, too.

Yet always hovering over the events of the war in his birth state is the almost palpable presence of President Abraham Lincoln. He admitted early that in the War Between the States he "must have Kentucky." Truly, Lincoln understood the strategic importance of the state as well as his counterpart, Jefferson Davis, also a Kentuckian by birth. If we are to truly grasp how much the state figured into his thinking and personality, we have to look at Lincoln's early life in the state, the role of former Kentuckians in his political and intellectual maturity, his love life with a string of Kentucky belles, and even the role of his Kentucky wife whose political acumen went far beyond the ordinary. While Lincoln may be the most written about person in American history, few biographers (Lowell Harrison, the notable exception) have truly understood the influence of The Bluegrass State on the man who knitted together again the torn and ragged fabric of the nation.

In the end, the stories of the Civil War in Kentucky, with its unique conglomerate of people and places caught in four years of chaos, will undoubtedly provide scholars and writers a rich vein of ore for many more years to come.

GREAT CIVIL WAR STORIES OF KENTUCKY

Lessons Lincoln Learned in Kentucky

Throughout our history, Americans have been fascinated by the early lives of our heroes.

We repeat the mythical Parson Weems story of the young George Washington cutting down the cherry tree and not lying about it when his father asks who, indeed, chopped it down. Or we carry in our collective memories the picture of the youthful Benjamin Franklin entering Philadelphia to find his fortune with a loaf of bread tucked under his arm, a sort of early American Horatio Alger. Or we sing about the legendary frontiersman Davy Crockett, who, "kill't him a bear when he was only three."

Likewise, there are stories about young Abe Lincoln: tales about his working for a neighbor, Josiah Crawford, for three days to pay off a debt for ruining a book by leaving it out in the rain, accounts of his wrestling matches with the pugnacious Clary Grove boys soon after arriving in New Salem as a young man, or the yarns about walking several miles to return a few pennies to a customer from his store that Lincoln had accidentally overcharged.

But these events happened in frontier Indiana and on the prairies of Illinois.

What do we know about Lincoln's days in Kentucky, his birthplace and home until he was about seven years old?

While Lincoln admits that he doesn't remember much about his life in Kentucky, recalling only his days at the Knob Creek Farm, the accounts of court records, several detailed biographies of his days in Kentucky, neighbors, and family do provide some interesting information about the young Railsplitter's days in The Bluegrass State.

And it was these events that in many ways helped shape and define him into the great man he became.

Psychologists tell us that our early years greatly influence the adults we become. Lincoln, then, was probably no exception

In fact, even at this young age, Kentucky left a lasting impression on Lincoln. So when young Lincoln left Kentucky in November of 1816 at the age of seven, he took with him lessons and impressions that guided him throughout his life.

On a farm his father bought in 1808, Abraham Lincoln greeted the earth at sunrise on Sunday, February 12, 1809, in a log cabin built by his father, located on Sinking Spring Farm, near the south fork of the Nolin Creek, just three miles outside of Hodgenville, Kentucky in what was then Hardin County, now Larue County. The elder Lincoln paid $200 to Isaac Bush on December 12, 1808, for what was eventually a 348-acre hardscrabble farm with a dark, open cave that trickled clear, cold water.

Peggy Waters, a twenty year-old neighbor, as quoted by local historian, John Lay, says that one of the greatest presidents in United States history was born on a bed of corn husks. "Nancy," Ms. Walters said in describing the birth, "has about a hard a time as most women, I reckon, easier than some and maybe harder than a few. It came along kind of slow, but everything was regular and all right."

The baby Abraham's father, Thomas Lincoln, who had plied his trade as a carpenter and cabinet maker, now struggled to support his wife, Nancy Hanks Lincoln, and his daughter, Sarah, by farming land too poor for crops.

But there appears to be much misinformation out there about Thomas Lincoln: that he was shiftless, lazy, good-for-nothing, that he would rather hunt than work, that he was a hopeless drunk—almost any human frailty that can be attached to a person, the elder Lincoln has been labeled.

Yet the public record does not support such a harsh condemnation of Abraham's father. For example, he paid cash for several of his farms. In 1814, in fact, Thomas Lincoln, born January 6, 1778 in Rockingham County, Virginia, ranked 16th in property value in Hardin County. He served on juries. He paid his taxes. He served as a bondsman for a wedding. In truth, he was well respected in the Elizabethtown community, a man who found no trouble finding work and from all indications an average citizen, working hard to support his wife and children.

A contemporary of his, Samuel Haycraft, described him as "a plain, plodding man [who] attended to his work, peaceable and good-natured, square built man of ordinary height."

A replica of the birth cabin of Abraham Lincoln near Hodgenville, Kentucky.

A replica of the cabin on the Knob Creek farm, Abraham Lincoln's second home in Kentucky.

Born February 5, 1784, near Brookneal, Virginia, Lincoln's mother, Nancy Hanks Lincoln, who married Thomas on June 12, 1806 in Washington County, Kentucky, has had similar publicity problems.

The most popular theory is that she was the illegitimate daughter of an unnamed prominent Virginia planter and Lucey Hanks, whose name later appears in early court records charged with immoral conduct. Later records show that Lucey later married Henry Sparrow, supposedly, to make things right.

In his book, *Lincoln's Parentage and Childhood*, Louis A. Warren and others advance another theory of Nancy Hanks Lincoln's paternity. Warren holds that Nancy was the daughter of the same Lucey, but rather Lucey Shipley Hanks and James Hanks, who died in North Carolina before Lucey migrated to Kentucky. Lucey then later re-married Henry Sparrow, for whom she was keeping house, and, according to other sources, was acting as his common law wife.

The charge of immoral conduct, supposedly, was an attempt by relatives to force her to marry Sparrow and thereby clear her name.

In other words, Lucey was married twice: once to James Hanks and later to Henry Sparrow. Her legitimate daughter Nancy, then, was the product of Lucey's first marriage to James Hanks. Warren cites certain court records to support his contention and explains that Abraham was fed false information from Dennis Hanks, an illegitimate cousin of his mother whose "facts" about the Hanks family were often questionable.

Abraham Lincoln himself, however, did think his mother was illegitimate, or so he confided to his law partner and later biographer, William Herndon. He told Herndon that his maternal grandmother was "shamefully taken advantage of by the man [the Virginia nobleman]. My mother inherited his qualities and I hers. All that I am or hope to be I get from my mother. God bless her." Lincoln explained that his analytical and intellectual powers came from what he thought was a prominent and highly intelligent, yet unknown Virginia grandfather.

Nancy Hanks Lincoln's parentage is a controversy that probably will never fully be resolved. What little we know about Nancy Hanks according to her biographers, Harold and Ernestine Briggs, was that she was "dark, with brown hair, gray eyes, strongly marked features, an accented chin and cheekbones, ...of slender medium height, quiet, and a little melancholy."

Lincoln later told Aminda Rogers Rankin, the mother of an Illinois businessman and friend of Lincoln, that "his instruction by her [his mother] in letters and morals, and especially the Bible stories, and the interest and love he acquired in the Bible through this teaching of his mother, had been the strongest and most influential experience in his life."

Apparently, life on the Sinking Springs farm was quite trying for Thomas Lincoln, for its thin, barren soil produced little the growing family could depend on. So when faced with eviction, because of competing claims for his property, suits so common in Kentucky at this time, he bought and moved to the 230 acre Knob Creek farm, ten miles away, in the spring of 1811.

It was here in a narrow, but rich black soil valley, surrounded by steep, but squatty hills with a clean stream running beside it, that young Abraham's memories of Kentucky began to accumulate.

Carl Howell, in his book on Lincoln's life in Kentucky, records an often-cited story about young Lincoln's near drowning. Austin Gollaher, four years older than Abe, claimed that once when he and Lincoln were playing near the rain-swollen Knob Creek, Abe accidentally fell in. Unable to swim, Gollaher grabbed a long pole, extended it to the floundering boy, and dragged him safely to the creek bank. According to Gollaher, Abe "was almost dead, and I was badly scared. I rolled and pounded him in good earnest. Then I got him by the arms and shook him, the water meanwhile pouring out of his mouth. By this means, I succeeded in bringing him to, and he was soon all right."

Lincoln himself recalled a particular planting there. He said, that the Knob Creek farm "was composed of three fields. It lay in the valley surrounded by high hills and deep gorges. Sometimes when there came a big rain in the hills, the water would come down through the gorges and spread all over the farm. The last thing I remember doing there was one Saturday afternoon. The other boys planted the corn in what we called the big field—it contained seven acres—and I dropped the pumpkin seeds. I dropped two seeds every other hill and every other row. The next Sunday morning there came a big rain in the hills. It did not rain a drop in the valley, but the water coming down through the gorges washed ground, corn, pumpkin seeds and all clear off the field."

Significant, though, was that the farm cornered on the Old Cumberland Road, a highway connecting the burgeoning cities of

Louisville to the north and Nashville, Tennessee to the south. While we cannot be certain, the chances are great that young Abraham witnessed passing groups of chained slaves, who had been "sold South," plodding wearily down the well-traveled road to unrelenting bondage.

What we do know for certain was that Thomas Lincoln did not believe in slavery, even though Hardin County had 1007 slaves at that time, so the young Lincoln must have seen hapless slaves in his visits for supplies in Elizabethtown and other parts of the county.

In fact, Thomas Lincoln was so adamant in his beliefs about slavery that he joined the nearby Little Mount Separate Baptist Church, known for its opposition to slavery. Young Abraham would have heard many fiery sermons that spelled out the wrong in owning other human beings.

Abraham later wrote that his father actually left Kentucky and moved to Indiana "partly on account of slavery." In the early 1850s, speaking of slavery to a young schoolboy, Abraham said, "I saw it all myself when I was only a little older than you are now, and the horrid pictures are in my mind yet." Later in his life, the president said that he could never remember a time when he didn't think, "slavery was wrong."

It was here in Kentucky that he learned that at an early age.

But Lincoln learned more pleasant things, too, in his early days in the Commonwealth. One of those was that he acquired the fundamentals of reading, a gift that served him well the rest of his life. Warren notes that Lincoln "was a product of the library rather than a child of the school," commenting on the generally self-taught Lincoln, who, while he may not have read extensively, did read deeply and quickly absorbed what he read.

Of course, he had to start somewhere, and that was in what was called an ABC school, where young students learned the fundamentals of reading. Many biographers say that it was a "blab school," a form of education where all children recited their lessons aloud, often at the same time. Indeed, Lincoln retained the habit of reading aloud the rest of his life. Many who witnessed his writing and speaking habits attest to Lincoln's reading a letter or speech aloud when preparing either.

Only about two miles from his home, near Athertonville, the school Lincoln attended was taught first by Zachariah Riney and then by Caleb Hazel for two sessions, in 1815 and 1816. Both were subscription schools, with tuition paid to the teachers by the parents of the students. Of the two teachers, Hazel, who, according to Howell, was a well-respected grammarian, probably more largely influenced the mind of young Abraham.

But teacher certification and state licensing were well in the future, so both men would probably be judged unqualified by today's standards. Yet his instructors did introduce Lincoln and his sister Sarah to the bare fundamentals of reading so that when he left Kentucky to move to southern Indiana, he packed three books for the trip: *Aesop's Fables*, the Bible, and *Dilworth's New Guide to the English Tongue*.

These three books were fundamental to Lincoln's later education, for he often quoted the Bible in his many speeches and letters. Many scholars say that Lincoln quoted scripture more than any president. In addition, he frequently used the tales from Aesop, along with his own yarns, as stories to illustrate points of law and sway the jurors.

The speller, of course, not only taught him spelling conventions, but also enriched his vocabulary, acquainted him with various well-turned phrases, and provided him the means for breaking down words into syllables. One contemporary, J.G. Holland, referring to Abe's pursuit of knowledge said, "No man ever lived, who was more a self-made man than Abraham Lincoln. Not a circumstance of life favored the development he had reached."

So by the time he left Kentucky, young Abe had already begun his dedicated pursuit of learning, a thirst he never was quite able to quench, despite his lifelong reading and writing.

He once told John P. Gulliver, a friend, a story to illustrate that idea. He said that after a visit from neighbors when he would hear words he didn't understand, that he would go to his bedroom and spend "no small part of the night walking up and down trying to make sense" of what they had said. "I could not sleep, though I often tried to, when I got on a hunt after an idea, until I had caught it."

Words, apparently, fascinated him. But his writing clearly indicates that he was not only enthralled by words, but he could use them well.

One last thing that Abraham Lincoln left Kentucky with was a lifelong dedication to the state and its people. Illinois may be the "Land of Lincoln," but the sixteenth president never quite left Kentucky behind.

Abraham Lincoln's love of words began very early in Kentucky. Courtesy of the Kentucky Historical Society.

All of his sweethearts were from Kentucky. From Caroline Meeker to Ann Rutledge to Mary Owens to Mary Todd, everyone was from The Bluegrass State. His "beau ideal" in politics was Kentucky's venerable Senator Henry Clay, the man who more than anyone shaped Lincoln's political thinking, his law partners, John T. Stuart, Stephen T. Logan, and William Herndon, were from Kentucky. His best friend, Joshua Speed, was from Kentucky. During the Civil War, Lincoln said, "I think to lose Kentucky is nearly the same as to lose the whole game." He is also reported as saying, that he hoped God was on his side, but he must have Kentucky. On several other occasions as president, he was uneasy about the effect of his Emancipation Proclamation on the Commonwealth. In essence, he fretted and worried about his birth state, never really getting Kentucky and its people out of his mind.

In November of 1816, with Abe nearly eight years old, tired of squabbles over ownership of his Knob Creek farm, and faced with eviction from his land once more, Thomas Lincoln and family packed what was necessary, and headed west for what was then Spencer County, Indiana, near present-day Gentryville, where they were surrounded by former Kentuckians also in need of free and title-clear land. Their route to the government plot of 160 acres probably included passing through Elizabethtown and Vine Grove (then called Viney Grove) in Hardin County, followed by Flaherty in Meade County and then onto Big Spring at the intersection of Meade, Hardin, and Breckinridge County. From there the Lincoln family made their way to Hardinsburg, before finally departing Kentucky on a ferry across the Ohio River, near Cloverport.

Young Abraham and his family may have left Kentucky behind, but Abraham Lincoln the man used what he had seen and acquired in the Commonwealth for the rest of his life. In fact, it's difficult to imagine how Lincoln, the Great Emancipator, the self-taught man, the lover of Kentucky and its people all his life, would become the man he did if he hadn't lived in The Bluegrass State in his early years, for all his life he was surrounded by Kentuckians, not by chance, but by choice. While he actually lived in the state for only seven years, for the rest of his life he seemed to have Kentucky and its people on his mind.

Lincoln, the Law and a Lady: A Kentucky Connection

In the fall of 1827, Abraham Lincoln, our sixteenth president, had a brush with the law that would be pivotal in persuading him to later become a lawyer.

The story of The Railsplitter's arrest and trial would be interesting enough alone, but this is a story involving a pretty young girl that the young Lincoln found quite alluring.

At the time Lincoln ran a ferry across the Anderson River, an Ohio River tributary, near Troy, Indiana, on the Ohio River, close to Lewisport, Kentucky in Hancock County, upriver from Owensboro a few miles.

Employed by a Green Taylor, the young Lincoln found out that he had quite a bit of time on his hands, so he decided to put some of his carpentry skills he had learned from his father to work by building a small, flat-bottomed row boat which he anchored in the Ohio River.

One day, two men came by and asked Lincoln to row them out to a waiting steamboat that could not reach the Indiana shore for fear of being grounded on a sand bar. Lincoln gladly consented, and as the two men boarded the steamer in the middle of the river, they both flipped him a shiny, silver fifty-cent piece for his efforts.

He later remarked that he found it all unbelievable.

The idea of, "a poor boy earning a dollar in less than a day" flabbergasted him, he told Secretary of State William Seward later.

Lincoln went on to say that he, "could hardly believe his eyes," and concluded that, "the world seemed wider and fairer." He later termed the event as, "a most important incident in my life."

Little did Lincoln know that two men on the other side were

watching him and plotting how to get their revenge on the strapping young Lincoln, who was convinced that his row boat had brought him an easy way to earn money.

On the Kentucky side, John T. Dill and his brother Lin operated a ferry across the Ohio River near land owned by Squire Samuel Pate, a wealthy plantation owner and magistrate, who often held court in his expansive log home situated a few hundred yards from the river.

In fact, the Dill brothers were operating under a license granted by the Commonwealth of Kentucky to run the ferry, which, in effect, forbade anyone else from transporting people across the river at that point.

The Dill brothers, then, saw Lincoln as violating the laws of Kentucky, and, perhaps, more importantly, as taking money out of their pockets. And this was not the first time Lincoln had done it, either.

Their intentions were to lure young Lincoln to their side of the river and give him a good ducking to remind him that he was cutting into their business and that they didn't appreciate it.

A portrait of Squire Samuel Pate, the magistrate who tried Abraham Lincoln and encouraged him to study law.

While Lin Dill summoned Lincoln to the Kentucky side by promising him business, John T. Dill hid in the bushes. After repeated calls Lincoln finally rowed to the Kentucky side to answer the bidding. He thought the person summoning him could not find the Dill brothers and needed help.

When Lincoln stepped out of his small boat, both Dill brothers grabbed him, but they soon realized that the sinewy six-foot four-inch Lincoln would probably be more than the two brothers could handle.

After a few moments of arguing, one of the brothers suggested that they take the young offender to Squire Pate for trial. Lincoln, believing that he had not committed any crime, consented reluctantly, and marched off to the nearby house of the young magistrate, Squire Samuel Pate.

Lincoln was arrested, charged with a penal offense, and summoned to court for a trial that began immediately.

The Dill brothers stated their case, content they would win since

Abraham Lincoln: He met up with the law in front of a Hancock County magistrate. Courtesy of the Kentucky Historical Society.

they were friends with Samuel Pate.

Known to take his job seriously, Squire Pate was about to find the defendant guilty, when Lincoln volunteered to speak. He asked the magistrate what the language of the law was. When the magistrate read the definition of a ferry, he discovered "ferrying" was defined as "setting persons across a river."

Lincoln pointed out to Squire Pate that he had not "set persons across a river," that, in fact, he had only taken those persons halfway across the river. Therefore, since he had ferried passengers only to the middle of the river, he had not technically violated the law.

Squire Pate realized that, indeed, Lincoln had a valid legal point, and directed a three-man jury to find Lincoln innocent of the charge. The Dill brothers sulked off while young Lincoln stayed to talk to Squire Pate, who complimented Lincoln on his budding legal mind. The magistrate encouraged Lincoln to study law and to return to observe other trials in Squire Pate's jurisdiction. He even offered Lincoln the opportunity to study his law books as part of his preparation, which Lincoln did on the Pate plantation.

But at the trial of Abraham Lincoln versus the Commonwealth of Kentucky there was at least one more person, Squire Pate's niece, Caroline Meeker, the orphan daughter of Squire Pate's sister, who stood in the open doorway during the proceedings.

According to the biographer William Barton, Caroline Meeker had curly brown hair, large expressive brown eyes, and a way about her that could capture almost anyone's attention. As Lincoln left the Pate house and walked toward the river, he passed through an orchard, his linen pants and shirt dressing out his massive frame.

Conveniently, Caroline was picking apples in the orchard when Lincoln hiked through. She offered him a shiny red apple, and commented on how happy she was that he had won the case. But she also dropped a hint that Eli Thrasher, a close neighbor and a brother of Pate's wife, was soon to have a corn husking party in his big barn, and she certainly would like to go to this gala event.

Young Lincoln took the hint, and offered to call for her the night of the party.

As the corn husking began, the judges separated the participants into two teams, with Lincoln and Miss Meeker on the same team.

The winner of the event was the team that husked the most number of ears of corn and that built up the larger pile of clean ears.

Tradition had it that if a young man found a rare red ear he could kiss any girl at the husking that he chose. Naturally, Lincoln kept his eyes focused on the pile of unhusked corn, hoping, just hoping, that he would find a red ear.

He didn't, but Caroline Meeker did and she slipped the red ear to young Lincoln. Lincoln complied with the tradition, legend has it, and kissed the fair Miss Meeker.

As Lincoln walked Caroline home, he began to reflect on himself and the beautiful Miss Meeker. He reasoned that he was certainly less than a match for the striking seventeen-year-old. She came from a wealthy plantation family, she was educated, and she deserved to marry someone of wealth and fine breeding.

Lincoln saw himself as a penniless pioneer, lacking in gentility and education, and pride. What could he offer the beautiful Miss Meeker?

In the end, he did not kiss again at her door.

But he did come back to the magistrate's court and learned law from the many trials that took place on "law days." And surely he did see Caroline again, but he soon sensed that Squire Pate's wife, Arretta, did not approve of the match, for she had designs on Miss Meeker marrying her brother, the wealthy Eli Thrasher, whom she considered a more appropriate match than Abraham Lincoln.

Mrs. Pate saw Lincoln as "too ugly" and not likely to "amount to much." She called him "Riverboat Abe," and "Driftwood Abe," among many unflattering names. But Squire Pate was much kinder, concluding that the young Lincoln had "a brilliant mind with strong determination but very little opportunity." Lincoln often read from Squire Pate's sixty-volume library, a large holding for that time and place.

Of course, Lincoln did continue to study law and became a

The grave of Caroline Thrasher, niece of Squire Samuel Pate, who showed a romantic interest in young Lincoln.

lawyer. Caroline Meeker did marry Eli Thrasher, but she died in childbirth on Christmas day in 1835, at the age of twenty-five. Barton notes that her husband Eli never fully got over Caroline's death and died himself a young man at thirty-nine. The daughter from the marriage was also named Caroline, but she died on June 2, 1851, just fifteen years old.

Lincoln's first contact with the legal profession began in Squire Samuel Pate's house near Lewisport, Kentucky. But, surely, in the years to come he must have reflected on his days at Squire Pate's house learning the fundamentals of his profession.

Surely, too, Lincoln must have wondered about that brown-eyed, brown haired beauty, Miss Caroline Meeker, his first "sweetheart," back in old Kentucky.

My thanks to Eli S. Gregory, great grandson of Squire Pate, for the major details of this story.

Lincoln's Poetry: A Look Inside

Kentucky-born Abraham Lincoln possessed an utter fascination with language that served him well throughout his life. As long as he lived he was able to use that ability in times of jest as well as in times of trouble. Indeed, his biographies are replete with descriptions of his masterful storytelling ability. And few who knew Lincoln well knew that, in spite of a squeaky and a decidedly Kentucky accent, he carried himself admirably in speaking of any kind.

But Lincoln, known for the soaring words of "The Gettysburg Address," also valued language in written form, too. In a lecture given in Springfield, Illinois on February 22, 1859, Lincoln remarked that "writing, the art of communicating thoughts to the mind through the eye, is the greatest invention of the world."

But his work was not limited to just writing speeches. He held a life-long fascination with poetry, regularly reading greats like William Shakespeare and Robert Burns and committing many lines to memory that he recited on numerous occasions.

But what most don't know is that throughout his life, he wrote poetry of his own that, while it doesn't mark him as a long-lost nineteenth century great American poet, it does help us to understand the man himself better. I've maintained the original spelling and punctuation to more accurately represent Lincoln the writer.

His earliest poetry dates to adolescence in a flippant piece of verbal gymnastics written sometime between ages 15 and 17:

> Abraham Lincoln
> his hand and pen

> he will be good but
> god knows When

The same copybook that provided the first piece also records these lines:

> Abraham Lincoln is my name[e]
> And with my pen I wrote the same
> I wrote in both hast[e] and speed
> And left it here for all to read

Such poetry hardly distinguishes Lincoln from others of the era who enjoyed showing off their verbal acumen, but it does show a young man who enjoyed seeing what he could do with language.

Yet even early examples of his poetry displayed the melancholy side of the man. While nineteenth century American poetry is filled with poems that trumpet the poet's fascination with death and dark despair, Lincoln's poetry seems, at times, <u>obsessed</u> with the pessimistic side of life.

The same copybook contains a poem built around this theme:

> Time What an em[p]ty vaper (sic)
> Tis and days how swift are swift as an indian arr[ow]
> fly on like a shooting star the prsant (sic) moment just
> [is here]
> then slides away in h[a]ste that we can
> never say they ['re ours] but [only say]
> th[ey]'re past.

In 1846, Lincoln attempted a much longer, more detailed exploration of his sentiments about his boyhood days in Indiana, prompted by a recent visit there on the campaign trail. The poem, entitled "My Childhood Home I See Again," begins with the stanza:

> My childhood home I see again,
> And gladden with the view;
> And still as mem'ries crowd my brain,
> There's sadness in it too.

The first stanza neatly sets the stage for what poets call an "apostrophe" to memory that follows:

> O memory! thou mid-way world
> 'Twixt Earth and Paradise,
> Where things decayed, and loved ones lost
> In dreamy shadows rise.

The stanza needs to be read within the context of some rather painful memories the young Lincoln had of his early days in Indiana where both his mother and beloved sister were buried, their lives cut short by the ardors of frontier life.

Michael Burlingame's penetrating study of the psychology of the man, *The Inner World of Abraham Lincoln*, notes, for example, that Lincoln's own words and the words of his favorite poets must have "reawakened memories of the painful losses he suffered as a youth."

Lincoln's own poem continues by noting that even these painful memories "seem hallowed, pure, and bright/Like scenes in some enchanted isle/All bathed in liquid light." He appears to be saying that in spite of the pain these memories bring him, they are still therapeutic to him in days of despair.

The fifth and sixth stanzas return to the transience of life theme:

> Where many were, how few remain
> Of old familiar things!
> But seeing these to mind again
> The lost and absent brings.
>
> The friends I left that parting day—
> How changed, as time has sped!
> Young childhood grown, strong manhood grey,
> And half of all are dead.

Subsequent lines reinforce this same theme until the poem takes an abrupt leap toward detailing the woes of a character Lincoln calls "Poor Matthew" who was "once a genius bright /A fortune-favored child" who now, because of mental illness had become "A haggard mad-man wild."

Given that Lincoln himself fought his own battles with what was then called "melancholia," and what we would now call clinical depression, writing these lines must have been quite painful for him, a pain he carried all his life.

After twenty-two stanzas, the poem begins what appears to be a whole new canto with a shift in emphasis to brighter subjects:

> And now away to seek some scene
> Less painful than the last—
> With less horror mingled in
> The present and the past.
>
> The very spot where grew the bread
> That formed my bones, I see.
> How strange, old field, on thee I tread,
> And feel I'm part of thee!

Unfortunately, the entire poem, if indeed there was more, has not been preserved. Lincoln makes an oblique reference to the poem in its entirety in a letter to Andrew Johnston on April 18, 1846, noting that the poem was "almost done." Yet the entire poem doesn't survive, and we don't know for sure that Lincoln even finished it.

But not all Lincoln's poetry was as depressing as this last piece. The victory at the Battle of Gettysburg on July 1-3, 1863, inspired Lincoln to put pen to paper in a piece called "Gen. Lee's Invasion of the North":

> In eighteen sixty three, with pomp,
> And might swell,
> Me and Jeff's Confederacy, went
> Forth to sack Phil-del,
> The Yankees they got arter us, and
> Giv us particular hell,
> And we skedaddled back again,
> And didn't sack Phil-del.

David Herbert Donald's Pulitzer Prize winning biography *Lincoln* says that Lincoln's enthusiasm inspired him to "compose a doggerel" that he quickly shared with John Hay, a secretary to the president. It was Lincoln, this time, using language to celebrate an important triumph, rather than bemoan his deep depression.

Lincoln's poetry probably will not survive on its own merits. It is often derivative and excessively maudlin, but reading it carefully provides insight into how one of our greatest presidents was also one of the most articulate presidents.

Abraham Lincoln and the Other Mary from Kentucky

In spite of his reputation as a plain or ugly man, the sixteenth president of the United States, Abraham Lincoln, still had a number of serious romances before he finally married Mary Todd on November 4, 1842.

But what is quite interesting about all of these relationships is that, except for Caroline Meeker, whom we know too little about to say, all Lincoln's ladies had a number of things in common. They were all from wealthy families. They were all far more educated than Lincoln. They were all slightly plump. Most were all relatively short in stature. They all, in one way or another, made him feel a bit insecure about providing for them financially.

And they were all from Kentucky.

To women in his day, Lincoln was not exactly a promising husband. In the company of educated women, he often stumbled around trying to think of something to say to women who felt at least comfortable being in the presence of eligible bachelors. Lincoln, of course, did not exhibit the same kind of ease around women that he felt around men. Around males, Lincoln had thousands of stories and jokes to tell, some a bit on the risqué side, and hardly suited for cultured young women who would have taken offense at any suggestion of impropriety.

His choice of clothing also reflected his rustic roots. He often appeared at parties and other social gatherings dressed in an ill-fitting suit whose trousers hit well above the ankles, what teenagers today called "high waters." Such pants often showed his long underwear and many times, even when he did wear suitable sartorial garbs, they looked much like he slept in them the night before. He often appeared with mud on his enormous boots. His ill-fitting suit covered a chest often described as much like a birdcage. Fond of wearing a hat, the hat grossly exaggerated his six-foot four-inch height all out of proportion. At such a height and weighing only about 180 pounds, most of his clothing did little to enhance his appearance.

Perhaps, part of that was that Lincoln was not a very handsome man. Besides having large ears and a prominent nose, Lincoln's neck was long and thin. He had coarse black hair that rarely was neatly combed, what some called later his "wild hair" that often showed up in formal portraits. His gray, pensive eyes belied the high speaking voice, some described as "squeaky," a voice often accompanied by awkward gestures made with large, sinewy hands. If that weren't enough, he spoke in a backwoods Kentucky drawl that contrasted sharply with the ladies he courted who spoke with careful attention to educated speech. He used phrases like "yonder way," and "cheer" for "chair" that reflected his lack of formal education.

Lincoln, in many ways, realized his less than dashing good looks—and made it the subject of self-deprecating humor. Once while riding the circuit as a young lawyer in central Illinois, he happened upon a woman in her yard staring intently at him. Curious, he stopped to see what she had to say. She looked him over, and announced, "You are the ugliest man I ever saw."

Lincoln, searching for an apt reply, said, "I know, madam, but there's not much I can do about it."

The woman replied curtly, "Well, you could stay at home more!"

In spite of his appearance, Lincoln persisted in his attempts to win a mate. The fact that he was thirty-three years old when he finally found someone to marry him attests to his struggle to find a bride.

Many people who knew Lincoln believed that he lost the one, true love of his life when Ann Rutledge died on August 25, 1835. At the time, Lincoln was living in the small Illinois village of New Salem, where Ann's father ran a tavern. Described as "beautiful and bright, "Miss Rutledge was born on January 7, 1813, near Henderson, Kentucky. Still a relatively young man of 22, Lincoln grieved so intensely after Ann's death that the small close-knit community feared that Lincoln would commit suicide, taking away his shaving razor from him, for example, they were so worried about him. He said once that he couldn't even stand the thought of it raining on Ann's fresh grave.

Early twentieth-century American poet, Edgar Lee Masters, has Miss Rutledge speak from the grave in these touching words:

> I am Ann Rutledge who sleeps beneath these weeds, Beloved in the life of Abraham Lincoln. Wedded to him, not through union, But through separation.

With the encouragement of his fellow residents, Lincoln, after a time, bounced back and began a curious relationship with a woman who had visited her sister in New Salem, in 1833, while Lincoln was still in the throes of the romance and subsequent death of Ann Rutledge. Her name was Mary Owens, born September 29, 1808, in Green County, Kentucky, the daughter of Nathaniel Owens and Nancy Grayham Owens. Records indicate that Mary S. Owens was from a prominent family, one of five children. Her father shows up on the tax rolls of the county as early as 1795; later information puts the size of the Owens land at 7,500 acres, a sizable plot of land for anyone to own.

Mary Owens: She was not impressed at all with Abraham Lincoln's courting. Courtesy of the Lincoln Presidential Library.

Although Baptist, Miss Owens received a good education at Nazareth, a Roman Catholic school near Bardstown, Kentucky in Nelson County. Years later, speaking about her father, Miss Owens remarked in a letter to William Herndon that, "few persons placed a higher estimation on education than he did." Her formal schooling and Lincoln's lack of it, like so many times before, was a factor in his not winning her hand.

Those who knew her describe her in various ways, with large variations in her height and weight. But most seem to agree on two words that picture her best: "handsome" and "smart." "Handsome," of course, is not a word we use now to describe a woman; we reserve it exclusively for men who fit the category. But "handsome" meant something different in Lincoln's day than it does today. Webster's Dictionary, published in 1828, defines "handsome" as "moderately beautiful," continuing "less than beautiful or elegant." That sense seems to be an accurate picture of Miss Owens. One source says, "she was tall, pretty, had large blue eyes and the finest trimmings I ever saw. She was jovial, social, loved wit and humor, had a liberal English education, and was considered wealthy." Another friend saw her as "truly handsome, matronly-looking, over ordinary size in height and weight." Several years later, in 1866, in a letter from Lincoln's biographer, Mary Owens herself says she is five feet, five inches and weighs about 150 pounds. "Tall" for woman in the early nineteenth century seems to mean something different than its present meaning.

The other word often used to describe her was that she was "smart." Other similar labels included "sensible" and "very intellectual," terms befitting a woman who had had a very good education for the times when sending women to school seemed to most fathers not a necessity at all. But one of her acquaintances, years later, said, "She was a very superior woman but like some other pretty women (God bless them) she loved Power and conquest." But he seems to be the only one who had that judgment.

At any rate, Miss Owens had a number of relatives in New Salem, and apparently she had made enough of an impression on young Lincoln that when her sister, Mrs. Betsy Abell, in the fall of 1836, told Lincoln that she was going back to Kentucky and returning with Mary Owens, Lincoln was interested. But, curiously, Betsy Abell went one step farther: She asked Lincoln if he would marry her.

Surprisingly, Lincoln said he would.

Mary S. Owens did return with her sister to New Salem. But Lincoln commented that she had lost some of her beauty in the three years since he had seen her, gained some weight, and seemed "a trifling too willing" to get married. One historian characterized Lincoln's reaction to the new Miss Mary Owens was that she "had grown stout and lost much of her comeliness."

But being the honest man of his reputation and having made a promise, Lincoln did court her.

Apparently, however, he did not make a very good impression. Perhaps, part of that was due to his misgivings about her, but he showed himself to be less than the gentleman she expected in a future husband.

She characterized their romance this way: "I thought Mr. Lincoln was deficient in those little links which make up the chain of a woman's happiness—at least in my case." She went on to explain herself: "Not that I believed it proceeded from a lack of goodness of heart; but his training had been different from mine; hence there was not that congeniality which would otherwise have existed."

What was it that made her feel that way?

Fact and legend swirl around two particular episodes in their relationship that may explain what she meant. As she relates it, once when she, Lincoln and some others were out for a ride they came upon what Miss Owens characterized as "a very bad branch to cross."

She continues: "The other gentlemen were very officious in seeing that their partners got safely over. We were behind, he riding in, never looking back to see how I got along. When I rode up beside him, I remarked, 'You are a nice fellow! I suppose you did not care whether my neck was broken or not!' He laughingly replied (I suppose by way of a compliment), that he knew I was plenty smart to take care of myself." For a woman of her breeding, Miss Owens thought this marked Lincoln as not the gentleman she was looking look for in a life mate.

There was still another time, although Mary Owens disputes that it ever came to words. She, her cousin Mrs. Bowling Green and her large baby, and Lincoln were walking over some rather rough country to the Abell's home, a distance uphill and nearly a mile. While Mrs. Green struggled to carry the oversized and fussy child, Miss Owens noticed that Lincoln never even offered to help carry the baby. As some tell the story, Miss Owens and Lincoln had an exchange of harsh words, but Miss Owens said she "gave little heed to the matter. We never had any hard feelings towards each other that I know of." One biographer described Lincoln in the matter as "attentive to Mary, but indifferent to the fatigue of the tired woman with the cross baby." It is probably significant that Mary Owens remembered the incident in such detail.

Lincoln and she continued to see each other for a time. But he had his doubts about the relationship, and she did, too. He managed to explain his feelings for her in a very interesting letter whose strategy seemed to be: You-want-all these-things, and I can't-provide-them-for-you, but if-you-really-want-to-get-married, well, all-right, I'll-marry-you.

He began: "You must know that I can not see you, or think of you, with entire indifference; and yet it may be, that you are mistaken in regard to what my real feelings are towards you are." He then assures her that, "I want in all cases to do right, and most particularly so, in all cases with woman." Lincoln then tells her that she can, "dismiss your thoughts (if you ever had any) from me forever, and leave this letter unanswered, without calling forth one murmur from me." In other words, Lincoln says, "that our further acquaintance shall depend on yourself."

He next tells her that she should not therefore feel that she is somehow bound to him: "Nothing would make me more miserable than to believe you miserable–nothing more happy, than to know you were so."

He then closes with: "If it suits you best to not answer this–farewell–a long life and a merry one attend you. But if you conclude to write back, speak plainly as I do."

He signs the letter: "Your friend Lincoln."—hardly a firm declaration of his undying love for her.

But, later, true to his word, he does ask her to marry him. She declined. Later, he proposed marriage to her once again. Again, she said no. And finally, for the third time he asked for her hand in marriage, and she turned him down for the third time.

She later explained herself gruffly, saying, "I suppose that my feelings were not sufficiently enlisted to have the matter consummated."

Here the story gets muddied a bit.

In a letter written two years later, on April Fool's Day of 1838 to the wife of a close friend, Lincoln seems to explain his relationship with Ms. Owens in terms not only unfavorable to Mary Owens, but also to himself. Was he just having fun in his letter to Mrs. Browning on a day when tomfoolery prevails? Or was he serious about how he discussed the romance with Miss Owens?

Both Mr. and Mrs. Orville Browning, the addressees of the letter, saw the letter as nothing more than an April Fools joke. But others have seen it as a truthful rendering of the romance.

In the letter, Lincoln describes Mary Owens as a "fair match for Falstaff," a corpulent, comic character out of one of Shakespeare's plays, who is described as being so fat that he "lards the lean earth as he walks along." Not much of a compliment for a lady Lincoln was considering marrying.

Lincoln then details Mary Owens' "withered features, for her skin was too full of fat to permit its contracting into wrinkles; but from her want of teeth, weather-beaten appearance in general, and from a kind of notion that ran in my head, that nothing could have commenced at the size of infancy, and reached her present bulk in less than thirty-five or forty years."

But since he had vowed he would make her his wife after all and live up to the bargain he made with her sister: "At once I determined to consider her my wife; and this done, all my powers of discovery were put to rack, in search of perfections in her...."

Yet Lincoln realizes that, "Through life I have been in no bondage, either real or imaginary from the thraldom of which I desired to be free."

But honor-bound, he says he asks her to marry him, and she turned him down. He then attests that "my vanity was deeply wounded... that I had so long been too stupid to discover her intentions."

He concludes: "Others have been made fools by the girls; but this can never be with truth said of me. I most emphatically, in this instance made a fool of myself."

Was Lincoln serious in describing his romance with Mary Owens? Or was the letter just a well-conceived April Fool's Day joke?

Somehow, there is a tinge of truth in it, it seems, for Lincoln didn't walk away unwounded. In fact, the last word Mary Owens ever received from Lincoln was in a message he told her sister, Mrs. Betsy Abell, to deliver to her: "Tell your sister that I think she was a great fool because she did not stay here and marry me."

When Mary Owens heard the message, she grumped, "Characteristic of the man!"

Their romance could be characterized as a relationship in which both could see that it just wasn't going to work out. She had her expectations, and he had his, and it was best that each went their separate ways. There might have been some egos bruised a bit, but neither would have been happy with the other one.

Mary Owens went back to Green County, Kentucky, married Jesse Vineyard, moved to Weston, Missouri, had five children, and died there July 4, 1877. Two of her sons fought for the Confederacy.

According to Herndon, shortly before she died, she was generous in her praise of Abraham Lincoln: "He was a man with a heart full of human kindness and a head full of common sense."

What better could she have said about an old romance that didn't blossom?

Lincoln's Last Visits to Kentucky

Abraham Lincoln and his family left Kentucky in November of 1816, when he was nearly eight, and moved to Pigeon Creek in southern Indiana, where his father, Thomas Lincoln, at last, had a clear title to his land, unlike the many problems he had had with three farms in Kentucky.

But the Kentucky-born president hadn't really left The Bluegrass State far behind. Many of his neighbors had migrated from Kentucky for the same reason as Lincoln's father. Kinfolk of the Lincolns, the Sparrows, found Indiana inviting, too, and soon built a cabin near the Lincoln's.

Young Abraham got his first taste of the law in Squire Samuel Pate's court, where he also met Pate's niece, Caroline Meeker, his first romantic interest, albeit as awkward as it was.

And when young Lincoln and his immediate family moved to the windy prairies of early Illinois in 1831 he still maintained many friends from the Commonwealth in the frontier settlement of New Salem and later in Springfield, where his law partners and romantic interests were from Kentucky, too. In fact, as far as we can tell, all of Lincoln's romances were with women from Kentucky, most of them well educated for their time and from aristocratic Kentucky families. Of course, his wife, Mary Todd, had strong Kentucky roots from a prominent family back in Lexington.

Kentucky, indeed, was never far from his mind.

As an adult, though, his trips to The Bluegrass State were limited in number, but near the end of his life, while in the White House, he expressed a fond desire to visit the state of his birth.

Farmington: Lincoln visited his closest friend, Joshua Speed, at this Louisville plantation.

The bed Abraham Lincoln is said to have slept in at Farmington, home to his friend, Joshua Speed.

His first visit was political in nature, when he was stumping for William Henry Harrison, the hero of the Battle of Tippecanoe, November 7, 1811, and the Whig candidate for president in the fall of 1840, the so-called Log Cabin Campaign.

Although he delivered a powerful speech that prominently mentioned Kentucky and Kentuckians on September 19, 1859, in Cincinnati, Ohio, Lincoln delivered his only political speech on September 8, 1840, in Morganfield, Kentucky, an Ohio River town with decidedly southern sentiments.

At the time, Lincoln, 31, honing his considerable oratorical skills in southern Illinois at Shawneetown, was an elector from Illinois. According to Louis Warren, one of the foremost authorities on Lincoln's early life, and Union County lawyer and local historian, George B. Simpson, Lincoln was lured to Morganfield by George W. Riddle, an important Union Countian and owner of a popular hotel known as "The Parson's House," located on South Morgan Street.

According to Simpson, two other prominent Whigs crossed the river with Lincoln. One was Samuel D. Marshall, a Yale educated and well-dressed son of John Marshall, a banker in Shawneetown. The other was Henry Eddy, founder of the Illinois newspaper, *Immigrant*, described as "influential in Illinois politics."

But the entourage didn't end there.

Twenty-six young women, dressed in finery and representing each of the states, crossed the Ohio in style in what Simpson describes as "a large canoe drawn by six white horses...along a band of singers, a hundred or so Whig party members in line, the local militia, women, children, and a cannon."

After a night in Riddle's hotel, amassing the unheard of bill of $30, the political celebrations the next day began with an elaborate parade of the band, young lasses, a drum and bugle corps and singers, all climaxing with the eager audience gathering around the speaker's platform for the much awaited political festivities. While there is no record of what Lincoln and his fellow Whigs said, the event began rather ominously when the cannon, backed up against a tree and whose roar was to begin the festivities, when lit, exploded into two pieces, and later became a part of local lore, with one piece ending up at the Kentucky Historical Society in Frankfort.

In those days when practiced orators learned to project their voices great distances, Lincoln's high, tenor voice, punctuated with his Kentucky drawl, must have easily carried to the awaiting listeners, eager to hear what this lanky lawyer had to say and how he said it.

Simpson rightly concludes, though, that because of the considerable presence of slaves in town, and as invited guests, probably "no abolitionists were present, nor was one word spoken concerning the abolition of slavery." Lincoln later learned in his run for U.S. senator that the southern part of Illinois, settled largely by Southerners, had different ideas about slavery than their northern neighbors.

What is left of an exploded cannon used during Lincoln's only political appearance in Kentucky. Courtesy of the Kentucky Historical Society.

What did Kentuckians Think of Lincoln?

It seems reasonable to think that in the crucial elections of 1860 and 1864, Abraham Lincoln, born near Hodgenville, would garner a sizeable number of votes in the Commonwealth. After all, he was a product of the Bluegrass State, who worked his hardscrabble beginnings into national prominence.

Couple that with the fact that his wife, Mary Todd Lincoln, was from a well-known and highly respected Lexington family, and that seems to add more evidence that Lincoln's popularity in Kentucky would be considerable.

In fact, in the 1860 election, in the entire state, Lincoln received a paltry 1,364 votes. In Fayette County, Mary Todd Lincoln's home county, only five people voted for him. In Lexington, her home town, he received only two votes.

In the election of 1864, in the middle of the Civil War, with Kentucky sending an ample number of Union soldiers into battle, Lincoln lost badly in the Commonwealth. In fact, the Democratic candidate, the impulsive and haughty former Union commander, General George McClellan, carried only three states: his home state, New Jersey, Delaware, and Kentucky. With many of Kentucky's Union soldiers supporting Lincoln, and with hints of voter fraud, Lincoln still lost with 26,592 votes to McClellan's 61,478. Even serving as a sitting president in a time of war, when most presidents easily win re-election, Lincoln received only 30% of the vote in Kentucky.

Considering that in this election, unlike the previous one, there were only two major candidates, while the 1860 election had four viable candidates, one of whom was another Kentuckian, John C. Breckinridge, and Lincoln's vote count in the second election indicates that The Railsplitter just wasn't very popular in the Bluegrass State.

Why?

Generally, present-day historians laud Lincoln for his policies and actions during this country's most trying time. Poll after poll of historians and political scientists place Lincoln as one of this country's most important presidents, if not right up there with George Washington.

Did Kentuckians of the time have legitimate complaints about Lincoln and his administration's handling of the War Between the States? After all, Kentucky was a slave state that chose to stay in the Union. Did Lincoln and his administration recognize and appreciate that?

In truth, the reasons for Lincoln's unpopularity in Kentucky are varied and many. But fortunately two lengthy studies of the times, William H. Townsend's *Lincoln and the Bluegrass*, and Lowell Harrison's *Lincoln of Kentucky*, although largely different in approaches, treat Lincoln's problems with Kentuckians in some great detail.

Several reasons for Lincoln's unpopularity stand out.

One explanation is that while Kentucky did permit slavery, except in the Bluegrass region and far western Kentucky, large plantations, tended by many slaves were the exception. Many people in the central region of the state plied at agriculture with just a few people in bondage, often just three or four. But the eastern mountainous region of the state, where plantations were rare, had few slaves. The Deep South, where large plantations used scores of slaves who worked in the acres and acres of cotton fields and who supported the way of life of a white aristocracy, was a perfect breeding ground for the fierce state's rights policies of plantation owners who reacted strongly at even a hint that their way of life was in jeopardy.

Yet, at the same time, Kentuckians believed they, too, had a right to keep slaves. After all, the Constitution guaranteed it, and Lincoln had promised that he would not interfere with slavery where it already existed, but they weren't willing to leave the Union over it. Kentuckians certainly had strong ties of blood and heritage to the rest of the South, but the state's citizens also engaged in vigorous trade with the North, especially just above the Ohio River where slavery was forbidden. In other words, the state's loyalties went both ways.

So at the outbreak of the war, Kentucky chose neutrality, meaning that she would not take sides in the irrepressible conflict, and asked governments North and South to respect her decision.

The Kentucky House of Representatives put it this way: "That this State and the citizens thereof should take no part in the civil war now being waged, except as mediator and friends to the belligerent parties; and that Kentucky should, during the contest, occupy the position of strict neutrality."

Obviously, such a position satisfied neither the Confederate government in Richmond, Virginia, nor the Union government in Washington, D.C. Lincoln wanted Kentucky in the Union, and Kentucky-born confederate President Jefferson Davis wanted Kentucky for the Confederacy, too. Each wanted Kentucky, then, as Harrison observes, because at the time the state was a very important state economically and politically, much more important than it is today.

Abraham Lincoln considered himself a Kentuckian, but Kentucky wasn't listening. Courtesy of the Kentucky Historical Society.

While both sides jockeyed for position in the state, both sides wooed the Commonwealth, often with rather obvious intent. The Confederates sent representatives to the state to stir up support, as did the Union, each side rallying forces with impassioned pleas and appeals to loyalty.

At the time, Lincoln summed it up this way: "I think to lose Kentucky is nearly the same as to lose the whole game. Kentucky gone, we can not hold Missouri, not, as I think, Maryland. These all against us, and the job on our hands is too large for us."

Justifying it as support for Kentuckians with strong Union sentiment, Lincoln sent Kentuckian William "Bull" Nelson into the state with five thousand guns, later called, for obvious reasons, "Lincoln guns." To many Kentuckians, even some of those who were Union in sentiment, such an act was a violation of Kentucky's neutrality. And it began a long series of events that seemed to signal to many in the state that Lincoln was going to force-feed the state the bitter pill of Unionism.

Later, even after the state did swing toward support for the Union cause and gave up its policy of neutrality, many Kentuckians were still left with the acrid taste of medicine in their mouths. Nothing symbolized such perceived mistreatment any better in the minds of its citizens than a series of military commanders who acted more like dictators than military officers sent to keep the peace.

While Kentuckian, General Jeremiah T. Boyle, and another Kentuckian, General John M. Palmer, and General Eleazor Arthur Paine did little to endear the Lincoln government in the minds of Kentuckians, General Stephen Gano Burbridge, a Logan County farmer, perpetrated so many egregious acts in the state that he became emblematic of all the Lincoln administration was doing wrong in Kentucky.

In his enthusiasm, Burbridge deleted the names of candidates in local elections in the state if they did not pass his tests for "loyalty." He censored bookstores for selling books that he thought would inspire loyalty to the Confederacy. He forced those not fully in support of the Union to pay for damages to property by Confederate guerrillas. He banished a Union war veteran who expressed disagreement with the policies of the Lincoln administration. He jailed the chief justice of Kentucky's Supreme Court and Judge Wiley P. Fowler of Graves County. He even jailed the lieutenant governor of the state, Richard Taylor Jacob.

But two of his policies were so outrageous to Kentuckians that even those who still supported the Stars and Stripes could not contain their hatred for the man.

One of those was the "Great Hog Swindle" in the fall of 1864 when Burbridge issued a proclamation that forced all Kentucky hog farmers to sell their surplus swine to an officer of the Union Army at what was deemed a "fair price." The "fair price" turned out to be considerably less than the farmers would receive on the open market. When farmers next tried to sell their hogs to markets across the Ohio River, especially in Cincinnati, known then as "Porkopolis" for all the pork processed there, Burbridge posted guards at the bridges, preventing hog farmers from selling their animals at higher market prices. Even Governor Thomas Bramlette, who had recommended Burbridge for the job, had had enough, and sent a scorching letter to Lincoln demanding the Lincoln vacate the order, which Lincoln did.

Yet, in the minds of the Commonwealth's citizens, the most galling insult inflicted by Burbridge was "General Order No. 59" that provided for the seizure of the property of those not loyal to the Union, the arrest and banishment of citizens not supporting the Lincoln government, and the lurid practice of selecting four Confederate prisoners of war to be shot in retaliation for every loyal Kentuckian killed by Confederate guerrillas.

Granted, guerrilla activity in the state was a real and everyday problem in the state. Guerrillas, some nothing more than criminals driven by bloody-eyed revenge, like Champ Ferguson, wreaked mayhem in many parts of the state, and Burbridge and Lincoln felt that they had to deal with the problem head on.

But many Kentuckians felt that Burbridge's measures went way too far.

In Meade County, for example, guerrillas murdered a loyal Union supporter and prominent farmer named David Henry. Burbridge promptly ordered the execution of four legitimate prisoners of war housed in Louisville. The hapless four were transported to the Henry farm, lined up, and summarily shot.

Had this been not an everyday practice, Kentuckians would have been more forgiving, but unfortunately, it wasn't. And the practice occurred again and again, all across the state, more than fifty executions in all.

One historian, E. Polk Johnson, writing more than forty years later, attributed Kentucky's decidedly Southern sympathies in the last days of the war and even after the war to "Butcher" Burbridge and his policies. In fact, after hostilities ceased, Burbridge was so unpopular in the state that he felt he and his family could not live safely there without fear of reprisal from its citizens. He died in Brooklyn, New York, still naively wondering why he was essentially banished from Kentucky.

In addition to Lincoln's suspension of habeas corpus in the state on July 5, 1864, allowing the government to hold prisoners without charge, still other policies of Lincoln angered Kentuckians. Several times, as Harrison details, the Lincoln administration had offered large sums of money to persuade Kentuckians to gradually emancipate their slaves. Although he had offered similar deals to several other Border States, he seemed especially intent on persuading Kentucky slave owners to give up human bondage. But slave owners stubbornly refused the president's offer.

So when Lincoln issued the Emancipation Proclamation on January 1, 1863, many Kentuckians felt that the Civil War really was, in Lincoln's mind, about freeing the slaves, not about saving the Union, as he had said earlier. Even Lincoln's closest friend, Louisvillian Joshua Speed, told Lincoln that the proclamation was a mistake. One Kentucky soldier in the Union army that Harrison quotes concluded that the document was "a most abominable, infamous document.... We find ourselves in arms to maintain doctrines, which, if announced 12 months ago, would have driven us all, not withstanding our loyalty to the Constitution and Union, into the ranks of the Southern army."

It is not surprising then, that when Lincoln approved enrolling black soldiers into the Union army that it was still another affront to Kentuckians. At first, Lincoln promised that none of the African Americans would serve in the state. But the exigencies of the war soon changed that, and Kentucky enrolled 23,703 black soldiers, more than any other state except for the militarily controlled Louisiana.

But, of course, all that manpower meant that Kentucky's economy would suffer, since slaves were largely used to harvest agricultural products. To encourage the recruitment of black soldiers, Lincoln ultimately offered not only freedom to the black soldiers, but also their families, further depleting the labor pool. It was just one more mark against the Lincoln administration.

There is a great deal of evidence that Lincoln's special regard for his birth state prompted him to proffer many favors to the state. Harrison even goes so far as to note that "the continued opposition in Kentucky to many of his policies caused him to devote attention there that could have well spent elsewhere."

So, in all fairness, though, Lincoln did attempt to mend fences in the state with gracious acts large and small.

One act is telling. Late in the war, on his last birthday of February 12, 1865, Lincoln met in the White House with Kentuckian Montgomery Blair, his former Postmaster General, who spoke with Lincoln about a letter he had received from a Versailles, Kentucky woman, Mrs. Martha Jones, the wife of a Confederate soldier, Willie Jones, whose husband was killed near Richmond. She pleaded with Lincoln to allow her, as she explained in her letter, to "visit his tomb, and the friends who attended his last moments, and receive his personal effects which are of sacred and inestimable value to me; and also permission to bring back from the South his man servant, whom I desire to manumit in consideration of his fidelity to his master." Enclosed in the letter, too, was a picture of the widow and the couple's daughter.

At first, Lincoln balked at granting her request, citing Union commander U.S. Grant's operations around Richmond, and the possibility that Mrs. Jones would reveal information to the Confederates about just what Grant and his army were doing.

But, then, as William Townsend tells the story, Lincoln laid the daguerreotype on his knee and studied it for a moment, then stared off at the fireplace, now crackling in the corner of the room.

"And, he never saw her again," and then repeated himself almost inaudibly.

Then, he got up and went to his desk and scribbled a short note that said, "Allow Mrs. Willis F. Jones to pass our lines with ordinary baggage, go South and return. A. Lincoln, February 12, 1865."

But apparently, news of his many acts of kindness like this one didn't make it to the majority of the state's citizen. After the war, from 1863 till 1891, Kentucky elected a series of governors who were either former Confederate soldiers or who had strong sympathies for the South. In addition, until recent times, the state has been a bastion of Southern Democratic politics, in part, some say, for what began as a repudiation of the policies of the Lincoln administration.

Yet as the memories of the great conflict slipped from the minds of its state's citizen and after generation gave way to succeeding generations, the Commonwealth began to think differently about the Great Emancipator. The opinions of Kentuckians underwent a change, turning from hatred and disgust to genuine appreciation, even veneration.

Now, in the state, Lincoln is rightly regarded as one of the Commonwealth's most distinguished products, symbolized, surely, by his statue's prominent place in the state's capitol rotunda. And the warm regards in the hearts of its people.

Henry Clay's Influence on Lincoln: The Lessons Lincoln Learned

Famous Kentucky Senator Henry Clay signed even important papers "H. Clay"; Abraham Lincoln signed his name as "A. Lincoln"; even documents like the Emancipation Proclamation were signed that way.

While it may be quite difficult to prove that Lincoln signed his name with just his first initial and last name because Henry Clay did, there are a number of other areas where Clay's influence on Lincoln's thinking and politics are, indeed, quite obvious.

Given Clay's stature in nineteenth century American politics that should not be surprising. For Clay was by almost all measures Kentucky's most distinguished politician. While Kentucky has had a number of important political leaders like John J. Crittenden, Alben Barkley, and John Sherman Cooper, none has matched Clay's influence on the state and nation like "The Sage of Ashland" or as he was also known "Harry of the West" or "Gallant Harry."

A committee headed by Senator John F. Kennedy in 1957 listed Senator Henry Clay of Kentucky as one of the five greatest senators in United States history.

And for good reason. Henry Clay seemed to possess all the skills requisite for an effective politician. He was an outstanding orator in a "Golden Age" of oratory along with the likes of Daniel Webster and John C. Calhoun, a time when speeches were sometimes several hours long, a form of entertainment in the early history of the United States.

He possessed a quick wit and charming personality that attracted people to him by the charisma he created. Over six feet in stature with piercing eyes and flawless manners, he drew people to him and seemed to bring out the best—and sometimes the worst—in them.

He seemed to have a knack also for political compromise, the ability to see common ground between two seemingly opposite positions and bring the two sides together in a civil manner. He is known by still another appellation as "The Great Compromiser" for his work in the Missouri Compromise of 1819-21, the Compromise Tariff of 1833, and his part in the Compromise of 1850, along with other important fence mending measures that avoided, at the time, what looked like a looming civil war.

And he voiced in word and action an undying faith in the purpose and destiny of the country, refusing to fall victim to the rabid sectionalism of some of his contemporaries. In an impassioned speech he concluded, "The Union is my country. The thirty states is my country...." "But even if it were my own state–if my own state, contrary to her duty, should raise the standard of disunion against the residue of the Union, I would go against her, I would go against Kentucky in that contingency as much as I love her."

When viewed through the lens of Clay's stature in the nineteenth-century political world, it should not be surprising that Lincoln in a speech in Ottawa, Illinois, during the famous Lincoln-Douglas senatorial debates, would call Clay his "beau ideal of a statesman, the man for whom I fought all my humble life." David Herbert Donald in his Pulitzer Prize-winning biography of The Rail Splitter goes a bit farther and says that Lincoln "almost worshipped Henry Clay." Edgar DeWitt Jones even wrote a treatise of some length entitled *The Influence of Henry Clay upon Abraham Lincoln*. Lincoln himself even characterized his politics as a brand of "old-line Henry Clay Whig."

An appropriate question, then, might be: In particular, what are some of the ways Henry Clay influenced the political thinking of Abraham Lincoln?

Senator Henry Clay: Kentucky's greatest senator, Abraham Lincoln's "beau ideal." Courtesy of the Kentucky Historical Society.

First, like Lincoln, Henry Clay was a "self-made man." In fact, Clay has been given credit for actually inventing the term itself. While Lincoln described his formal education as being less than a year, or as "by littles" as he called it, Henry Clay's was not much longer. Melba Porter Hay, in an entry in the *Kentucky Encyclopedia*, characterizes Clay's early education as "rudimentary" but notes that Clay continued his education under the tutelage of George Wythe, "a classical and law professor," who "directed [Clay's] studies, giving Clay his mastery of the English language." In an age when the chances of a poor Indiana farm boy getting a good education in backwoods schools were slim, Lincoln must have been quite encouraged by his model and all that he had done with his meager education. With a burning desire to educate himself, Clay's prominence not only in politics but also his influence on the very fabric of the nation would be a beacon for Lincoln's lofty ambitions.

Second, Clay almost surely influenced nascent belief in what is normally called Clay's "American System." Basically, an economic road map for the young nation, the American System revolved around three interrelated policies that the Kentucky senator thought spelled progress for a nation just getting on its economic feet after the War of 1812. Based in large part on the thinking of Alexander Hamilton, the country's first Secretary of the Treasury, the American System advocated protecting the young industrial growth of the United States by high tariffs that would increase the cost of consumer goods bought from other countries. Such a policy was thought to give the fledgling industries in the country a chance to grow to the point that they could provide the citizens with the manufactured goods so necessary for the country's economy.

Both the 1856 and 1860 Republican Party platforms that Lincoln so enthusiastically endorsed contained planks that advocated protective tariffs.

Another part of Clay's plan called on the United States government to use the monies generated from the sale of public lands to tackle projects for internal improvements, things like dredging rivers to make them more navigable, building canals and roads so that farmers and young entrepreneurs could get their goods to markets far from their farms and factories. Clay argued, like many present-day politicians, that the economy of the nations depended on the accessibility of the creator of the goods and services to the market; this was vital to economic growth.

Lincoln agreed. In 1832, Lincoln launched his political career by running for a seat in the Illinois legislature. In his campaign, he pledged to work toward improving the river navigation on the Sangamon River that ran through his district. He felt that by making commerce on the river possible, his district would prosper. It was the kind of pledge that other Whigs, influenced by Clay's plan, were advocating around the country. Once again, both the 1856 and 1860 Lincoln's Republican Party platform advocated internal improvements like a railroad to the Pacific coast and "the improvement of rivers and harbors, of a national character, required for the accommodation and security of our existing commerce."

The third prong in Clay's American System was his advocacy of a national bank which would both issue currency and underwrite the financing of projects vital to the American economy, creating, in the process, what one economist calls the "financial infrastructure" for the young nation. Clay and Lincoln alike felt that the nation needed to have its source of money. During the Lincoln administration, the Legal Tender Act of 1862, which authorized the issuance of paper money, and the National Banking Act of 1863 proved to be an outgrowth, in large part, of Clay's thinking several years prior.

Although Clay represented a Southern state, his American System was largely unpopular in the South. Southern planters and other important Southern leaders fought for a system that collected a minimum amount of tariffs since their economy depended on providing countries like England with raw exports like cotton, hemp, and tobacco. In fact, in 1830, South Carolina sought to nullify a federal law that called for the collection of duties that South Carolinians felt unjustly impinged on their economy. Indeed, South Carolina threatened to secede from the Union over the crisis, since she felt she had the power to "nullify" a federal law that didn't operate in her interest. Clay once again used his ability to find a compromise solution to the crisis. Largely agricultural in nature, the Southern economy also did not see the need for internal improvements that much of the rest of the country wanted. In the end, the Nullification Crisis was a precursor to events some thirty years down the road in a South Carolina harbor, a place called Fort Sumter.

Although not generally known by the American people, Clay also greatly influenced Lincoln's thinking about the question of slavery and what the country should do about it. Although he did indeed own slaves, Clay advocated the abolition of slavery. He once said: "I have ever regarded slavery as a great evil, a wrong, for the present I fear, an irremedial wrong to its unfortunate victims. I should rejoice if not a single slave breathed the air or was within the limits of our country." Lincoln, of course, also believed that slavery was wrong, once remarking, "slavery was wrong, morally and politically." While Lincoln did not suffer the stigma attached to Clay, who, on one hand, advocated the emancipation of slaves, while, on the other hand, did own slaves, a fact that may have, according to some historians, cost Clay the presidency, Lincoln shared similar views on what to do about slavery.

Both Clay and Lincoln ardently believed that freeing the slaves and allowing them to integrate into American society was not the answer. Some historians have argued that both men did not think it was possible for freed slaves to function in American society because of the rampant prejudice in American society toward them. In 1845, Clay remarked, "in whatever mode the U.S. may get rid of the Free Blacks, I believe it is better for them and for the whites." Historians remind us that this is the period in the nation's history where nativism, the belief that America was for white people, particularly Protestants, was very much a part of the belief system of many Americans. Even Midwesterners feared that if freed slaves were allowed free access, they would threaten the jobs of white people. Some citizens believed that keeping slavery in effect where it already existed guaranteed their economic prosperity so that not freeing them was a workable solution to the problem. Truly, they clung tenaciously to their position. For example, both Indiana and Illinois had laws that prohibited freed Blacks from residing in the state. Both Clay and Lincoln, then, were aware of the attitudes towards African Americans in various parts of the nation.

The answer to the slavery problem, as these two men saw it, was the colonization of freed slaves in Africa. Basically, the thinking of those advocating colonization was that gradually slaves would be emancipated by their masters, either by reaching a particular age or by buying their freedom from their masters. These freed slaves would then be shipped to particular parts of Africa, specifically Liberia, where they would return to their Mother Land, use the skills they had learned while in captivity, and prosper as free citizens. Clay, in fact, was one of the founders of the American Colonization Society, organized on January 1, 1817, with the expressed purpose of "ameliorat[ing] the condition of the Free people of Color now in the United States, by providing a colonial retreat, either on this continent or that of Africa." Clay served as the organization's president for twenty-six years.

Lincoln enthusiastically agreed with Clay's solution to the slavery problem. In his eulogy for Clay, Lincoln noted that "if as the friends of colonization hope, the present and coming generations of our countrymen shall by any means, succeed in freeing our land from the dangerous presence of slavery; and, at the same time, in restoring a captive people to their long-lost fatherland, with bright prospects for the future; and this too, so gradually that neither their races nor individuals shall have suffered by the change, it will be indeed a glorious consummation." Lincoln even went on to say that in regard to Clay's efforts in this area "none of his labors will have been more valuable to his country."

But, of course, the colonization movement never really caught on in the Deep South where slaves were too valuable to the Southern economy to give up to the colonization movement.

As Michael Lind notes in his book on Lincoln's beliefs, some have argued that before his death, Lincoln abandoned his support for the colonization idea. Lincoln's secretary, John Hay, in a July 1, 1864 entry, wrote: "I am happy that the President has sloughed off that idea of colonization." But General Benjamin Butler claimed that Lincoln asked him to "carefully examine the question and give me your views upon it and go into figures, ...so as to show whether the Negroes can be exported." One old friend of Lincoln, in 1892, said, "Lincoln was a colonizationist, as Jefferson, Madison and Henry Clay were."

The question probably will never really be answered, but it appears quite obvious that Lincoln, in so many ways, borrowed much of his political thinking from the venerable senator from Kentucky, Henry Clay.

Years after Clay had died, on August 9, 1862, Lincoln wrote Henry Clay's son, John, to thank him for giving Lincoln the venerable senator's snuff box. Lincoln even then could hear Clay speaking to him: "I recognize his voice," Lincoln said, "speaking as it ever spoke, for the Union, the Constitution, and the freedom of mankind."

Kentucky's Senator John J. Crittenden: His Attempts to Prevent the Civil War

While most Kentuckians know that both Abraham Lincoln, President of the United States; and Jefferson Davis, President of the Confederate States of America, were born in Kentucky, few know about another important Kentuckian and his role in trying to prevent the national bloodbath called the Civil War.

Even though his efforts were unsuccessful, that does not diminish the great zeal and fervent dedication that this son of Kentucky showed in doing all he could do to keep the Union together, for he realized all too well that the country was headed for its greatest crisis.

John Jordan Crittenden was born on September 10, 1786, near Versailles, Kentucky. He attended what later became Washington and Lee College, but graduated from William and Mary in 1807, served as territorial attorney of Illinois, but returned to Kentucky before the War of 1812, and worked as an aide to Governor Isaac Shelby.

Crittenden was elected to several terms in the Kentucky legislature before serving in the United States Senate off and on from 1817 through 1861, pausing very briefly to become United States Attorney General in President William Henry Harrison's cabinet, but resigned shortly thereafter over the issue of the national bank when President John Tyler assumed the presidency after Harrison's death. Crittenden also served as Attorney General in the Millard Fillmore administration.

Politically a Whig, later a Know-Nothing party member, and finally joining the Constitutional Union Party, Crittenden's political skills were great.

Blessed with a commanding presence, piercing dark eyes, and a resonant voice, Crittenden was a very persuasive speaker. After his death, one senator, J.F. Bell, described his speeches in the Senate as having a "magic influence imparted to his genius by generous emotions, contempt for meanness, hatred for wrong, admiration for loftiness of purpose, and an unyielding spirit to uphold the right. In his political and senatorial debates he was quick with apprehension, clear in statement, eloquent and earnest in argument; always candid, never seeking an advantage at the expense of truth; unambitious, forgetful of himself; and above all, truly patriotic, ever looking to his country's good."

Kentucky Senator John J. Crittenden tried to prevent the war. Courtesy of the Kentucky Historical Society.

In the events of December of 1860, Crittenden would need all those rhetorical and political skills as he set about the task of trying to prevent what one contemporary of Crittenden, Senator William Seward of New York, called the "irrepressible conflict."

In truth, Crittenden was the natural choice to work toward some sort of compromise. As historian Patsy S. Ledbetter points out, first, he was from Kentucky, a border state that had political and economic ties that ran both North and South.

Second, he also understood slavery as an institution in the South, and he comprehended the North's revulsion of the same institution.

Third, in the eyes of many, Crittenden also wore the mantle of the Great Compromiser himself, the revered Kentuckian, Henry Clay, whose work on the Compromise of 1820 and Compromise of 1850 certainly may not have prevented the Civil War but surely delayed it for several years. Fourth, Crittenden had the advantage of being a member of neither the Republican nor the Democratic Party at this point in the crisis. In Ledbetter's words, "since he represented the middle ground both geographically and ideologically, if a mutually acceptable position was feasible, hopefully he could find it."

In the days between Lincoln's inauguration and the end of President James Buchanan's administration, Buchanan, hoping to defuse the impending crisis, sent a message to Congress, suggesting that perhaps a series of constitutional amendments might prevent war.

On December 6, 1860, another Kentucky senator, Lazarus Powell, introduced a bill to form a committee of thirteen members, composed of senators from the North and South, including five Republicans from the North and West, five Southern Democrats, and three Northern Democrats who were to mediate between the Republicans and the Southerners. Among the committee members were William Seward, later Secretary of State in the Lincoln administration; Robert Toombs, later Secretary of State for the Confederacy; Stephen A. Douglas, Lincoln's old political rival and later presidential candidate in 1860 for the Northern Democrats; and, most notably, Jefferson Davis, later president of the Confederate States of America.

The thirteen member committee was charged with the responsibility of determining the controversial issues facing the country, considering legislation that might ease tensions, and offering possible constitutional amendments that would help to hold the country together.

After much political wrangling and posturing, Georgia Senator Alfred Iverson announced that "all these devices to stay the storm which now rages in the southern states, to prevent that people from marching on to the deliverance and liberty to which they are resolved, but sir, the words 'too late' that ring here today will be reiterated from mountain to valley in all the south."

But on December 18, in spite of delaying tactics on both sides, the proposal to set up the committee passed on the Senate floor.

Crittenden was ready, and immediately offered his plan to calm the storm over the land.

He proposed a six-part solution.

First, he advanced the idea that the Missouri Compromise line of demarcation, 36' 30' be extended all the way to the Pacific Ocean. South of that line, slavery would be allowed, and any future states in that territory would decide whether or not to be a slave state or a free state by popular vote of its citizens.

This proposal, the most controversial, was aimed at satisfying the South.

Second, Crittenden proposed that Congress could not abolish slavery where it already existed.

Third, the Kentucky senator suggested that slavery in the District of Columbia could not be abolished at any time unless Maryland and Virginia freed their slaves or until the majority of citizens of the district voted for emancipation.

Fourth, Crittenden moved that Congress could not interfere with interstate slave trade.

Fifth, the senator proposed that slave owners be compensated for runaway slaves not returned under the terms of the Fugitive Slave Act, which required their return.

Sixth, Crittenden sought to again allay the fears of the South by declaring in his compromise "no future amendment to the Constitution shall affect the five preceding articles." In other words, the Crittenden Compromise was set in stone.

Crittenden's biographer, Albert D. Kirwan, explained that the Kentucky senator thought "he had looked impartially from section to section in order to seek out the causes of discontent as well as the means to remedy them."

Crittenden saw his compromise not as an issue of being Republican or Democrat, but the greater issue of what he called "the life of this great people." To him, to dissolve the Union represented "the greatest shock that civilization and free government have received."

Compromise, he said, was the "cheapest price at which such a blessing as this Union was ever purchased." He urged Democrats and Republicans alike to accept his proposals so that "we shall go again in our great career of national prosperity and national glory."

But when the compromise finally came up for vote, the plan Crittenden worked so hard and long for was defeated.

Even the President-elect, Abraham Lincoln, could not support Crittenden's plan.

Why would Lincoln, who later referred to the awful "scourge of war," not support a plan to possibly avoid the Civil War?

Historian Isaiah Woodward, writing to answer that question, maintains that Lincoln and the Republican Party platform he was elected on was resolutely against any proposal that extended slavery into the territories not yet organized into states.

Lincoln said he would "entertain no propositions for compromise in regard to the extension of slavery. I am for no compromise that assists or permits the extension of the institution on soil owned by the nation. And any trick by which the nation is to acquire territory and then allow some local authority to spread slavery over it is as obnoxious as any other."

He then dismissed the Crittenden Compromise as putting the nation "on the high road to a slave empire."

Certainly, the President-elect's stand on the compromise was crucial to its success. But why, with the fate of the United States at stake, couldn't the parties agree? After all, it surely could have avoided civil war?

While some might blame Lincoln, and others assign guilt to the politicians who would not rise above partisan politics, one observer explains it still another way.

Walter R. Fisher looks at the reason the Crittenden Compromise failed as a problem with rhetoric, the art of persuasion.

Fisher sees various reasons the parties could not agree on this measure to avert war.

First, he notes that the North and the South had two different conceptions of what the United States was. That is quite important because how each side <u>saw</u> the Union affected the way they looked at <u>maintaining</u> it.

The South saw the United States as a <u>compact</u>. John Hemphill of Texas said that the compact is "a frame of government for those upon whom it operates; and the states being sovereign members of this league . . . have a right, as stable as the foundation of international law, to renounce the league at any time, and withdraw from the federation."

So the United States, to the leaders of the South, was just a loose arrangement of states, entirely to themselves.

The North saw it differently. To them, the United States was a <u>contract</u>, a union indivisible, not capable of being dissolved. Lincoln, for example, thought that way, always referring to the Confederate States of America, not as the C.S.A., but as the "states in rebellion."

Crittenden's Compromise failed, in part, then, because Crittenden assumed that both sides wanted to maintain the "glorious Union."

Yet the South didn't see it as a union at all, but a convenient compact.

Secondly, Fisher says the compromise failed because the South was convinced that the North "was hostile to southern institutions," slavery, and their whole way of life that was built on a culture quite different from the North.

In other words, when both sides feel that the other side is not acting in good faith, then compromise is unlikely, especially when one side, the South, felt the North was trying to destroy their way of life. Jefferson Davis expressed this idea well: "Between oppression and submission to power, we will invoke the God of Battles, meet our fate, whatever it may be."

Third, Fisher says the compromise failed because the Republicans and Democrats alike were not budging on the question of the extension of slavery.

The Republicans saw the issue of slavery as a moral question. Their hatred of slavery was so strong that they would not even entertain any notion that might lead to more slave states. They saw slavery, then, as a terrible cancer on the body politic. Lincoln's remarks were typical of the Republican stand.

On the other hand, the South saw slavery as an institution at the very foundation of their agrarian society. As they viewed it, the Bible sanctioned slavery, and, besides, slaves were property that the North was trying to take away.

As Fisher concludes, "concession of southerners or northerners on these first principles involved a surrender not only of political power and prestige but also of integrity, of fundamental precepts, of rival ways of life."

In another context, biographer Benjamin Thomas noted that when a controversy is over moral issues and each side sees itself as having "right and justice on their side (as both the North and South did), then there is no further hope of compromise."

That fits the context of the Crittenden Compromise quite well.

After the Crittenden Compromise failed in Congress, Senator Crittenden tried other ways to revive interest in it, even attending the Peace Convention, convened by the state of Virginia to avoid the looming crisis. He offered his help in that meeting's success. In fact, he seemed willing to do almost anything to avoid war. But, of course, the Peace Convention failed to avert war, too.

Ultimately, frustrated by the unwillingness of the North and South to compromise, he concluded that "We fall with the ignominy on our heads of doing nothing, like the man who stands by and sees his house in flames, and says to himself, 'perhaps the fire will stop before it consumes all.'"

Crittenden himself called the defeat of his compromise the "darkest day" of his life. Kirwan described the same event as "the great tragedy of his life."

The noble Kentuckian who had so relentlessly pursued peace had failed.

But in spite of that, he deserves both recognition and respect for all he tried to do to bring tranquility to a troubled land.

His biographer says that on July 26, 1863, John J. Crittenden died "quickly and with little suffering," nearly two years before the end of the war he fought so hard to avoid.

Ironically, Crittenden had two sons who fought in the war: both major generals: Thomas, who fought for the Union; and George, who fought for the Confederacy.

Confederate General Ben Hardin Helm: A Promising Kentuckian Dies Too Young

At the outbreak of the Civil War, few men in Kentucky showed more promise than Ben Hardin Helm, son of former Kentucky Governor John LaRue Helm and Lucinda Barbour Hardin.

The recipient of a good education, and blessed with a winsome disposition, at the time of his death young Helm looked assuredly like a man who would follow in his father's footsteps to, if not state, perhaps even national office.

He was, after all, the brother-in-law of President Abraham Lincoln.

Born at the home of his grandfather in Bardstown on June 2, 1831, young Helm grew up in Elizabethtown in a family of twelve children and attended Elizabethtown Seminary for what his biographer R. Gerald McMurtry calls his "literary education." Being quite precocious, he completed the curriculum well ahead of schedule at the age of fifteen.

From there, Helm attended Kentucky Military Institute for just three months before entering West Point on July 1, 1847, graduating ninth in a class of forty-two in 1851. He also attended the Cavalry School for Practice at Carlisle, Pennsylvania for advanced training before being assigned to the frontier at Fort Lincoln, Texas as a second lieutenant.

While serving in Texas, he developed inflammatory rheumatism, which made his life as a professional soldier very difficult. He returned to Kentucky after only six months of active duty, convinced, however, that, if at all possible, he wanted to be a professional soldier, longing, as McMurtry says, "for the day when he could rejoin his comrades at Fort Lincoln," but ultimately forced to resign his commission on October 9, 1852.

Realizing that he had to turn to other ways of making a living, Helm chose the study of law, graduating from the University of Louisville School of Law in 1853. He then entered Harvard University Law School for a six-month course, and returned to practice law with his father.

In 1856, he organized a practice with Martin H. Cofer for about two years before setting out for Louisville where he set up a practice with Horatio W. Bruce, his brother-in law. Helm soon set himself apart from most lawyers in Louisville, displaying what McMurtry calls "a high sense of honor" and "unswerving integrity" which earned him the reputation as "one of the ablest lawyers practicing before the Kentucky courts." His reputation was of a man who used both his military training and his law school education to render blistering refutations to those who sat across from him.

General Ben Hardin Helm, C.S.A.: Lincoln's brother-in-law with a promising career cut short. Courtesy of the Kentucky Historical Society.

Yet besides his success as a lawyer, he also had a career as an up and coming politician in those days when politics commanded more respect and distinction. In 1855, at just twenty-four, he was elected to the Kentucky General Assembly as a representative from Hardin County. He later also served as the Commonwealth Attorney from the Third District from Kentucky.

While serving in Frankfort, he met Emilie Todd, daughter of Lexingtonian Robert Todd, and half-sister of Mary Todd Lincoln, wife of the sixteenth President. Helm and Emilie Todd were married in Frankfort on March 20, 1856, with a grand reception in Southern style at the home of the Todds.

Abraham Lincoln met his new brother-in-law while Helm was visiting Springfield to argue a case in the Illinois capital. The men developed a distinct fondness for one another, a friendship that would develop into a fateful decision for Helm just a few short years later. In spite of their sharp political differences (Lincoln was a Henry Clay

Whig turned Republican while Helm was a staunch state's rights Democrat) the two men had much to talk about.

As McMurtry points out, Lincoln and Helm chatted often about Elizabethtown, the former home of Lincoln's parents, Thomas and Nancy Hanks Lincoln, and the small town of Hodgenville, near the site of Lincoln's birth.

Yet in spite of the warmth between them, Helm did not campaign for his brother-in-law, choosing instead to work for John Bell, the candidate of the Constitutional Union party. Even though he and Lincoln were relatives by marriage, Helm still maintained his Southern sympathies.

After Lincoln's election, Helm felt that there would be no war, for he held faith that the Union would not dissolve. When events proved otherwise, Helm volunteered to be Inspector General of the Kentucky State Guard under General Simon Bolivar Buckner in an effort to defend Kentucky's neutrality.

Not knowing at the time where his true sentiments lay, Helm made a visit to Washington to consult with Lincoln.

As their conversation came to a close, Lincoln gave Helm an envelope and asked Ben to "think it over" and let the President know what his answer was.

When Helm opened the envelope, he discovered that Lincoln had offered him, along with the rank of major, the paymaster position for the Union army, a coveted, noncombatant job sure to keep him out of danger. Lincoln reasoned that with Helm's West Point education and his further training in the law, the paymaster job would be well suited to the young Kentuckian's strengths.

As McMurtry relates it, Helm sat down and wrote Lincoln a long letter: "The position you offer me is beyond what I had expected in my most hopeful dreams. It is the place above all others which suits me." Helm continued: "I have no claim upon you, for I opposed your candidacy and did what I could for the election of another." But he ended: "I try to do what is right," and with that he turned down Lincoln's offer on April 27, 1861.

So when Kentucky's neutrality was challenged and the state legislature took on a decidedly Union cast, after talking to Buckner and his friends, including Robert E. Lee, Helm chose to side with the Confederacy.

Helm found President Jefferson Davis in Montgomery, Alabama, and offered his service to the Confederate cause. Curiously, Davis told Helm that he didn't really need anymore soldiers then, and advised Helm to return to the Bluegrass State and try to secure the Commonwealth for the South.

But, of course, it was too late for Kentucky to join the Confederacy. Not to be deterred, Helm organized the First Regiment of the Kentucky Cavalry, composed of ten companies of loyal soldiers in gray. Earning the rank of colonel, Helm mustered in at Bowling Green, Kentucky and organized the regiment on October 19, 1861.

He quickly set about the task of training the men for combat with numerous sabre drills and other exercises designed to ready his men for combat. His men took to him quickly and acknowledged that Helm knew his military tactics well.

When Helm and his regiment reached Murfeesboro, Tennessee on February 23, 1862, the first duty they were assigned was a reconnaissance foray under fellow Kentuckian General John C. Breckinridge near Corinth, Mississippi, close to the site of the Battle of Shiloh.

Soon the First Regiment pulled similar duty under famed General Albert Sydney Johnston. Johnston, who was acting on Helm's observations, planned to attack the opposing General U.S. Grant before Union General Carlos Buell arrived with reinforcements. But Buell had already arrived and his force along with Grant's spelled defeat for the Confederate forces.

Even more significant, the Gray Clads lost the services of perhaps their best-trained and most experienced generals, Albert Sydney Johnston, who was killed at Shiloh.

But overall, Helm's men performed admirably, and Colonel Helm became Brigadier Helm officially on April 17, 1862, backdated to March 14, 1862.

After commanding the Third Brigade of the Reserve Corps for a short time, Helm was then assigned as commander of the Second Brigade, a unit consisting of men from Alabama and Mississippi, along with fellow Kentuckians.

McMurtry, tracing Helm's intricate movements, has Helm and his men next assigned duties in Louisiana, particularly Baton Rouge, where a series of tragic mistakes led Helm's men to mistakenly fire on their own comrades. Compounding that, Helm was thrown from his horse, suffering injuries that put him out of action until

September, when Helm was transferred to Pollard, Alabama to the command of General William Joseph Hardee. Ultimately, once again he served under Breckinridge, where Helm in February of 1863 assumed command of the First Kentucky Brigade, the famous "Orphan Brigade." After serving in the Vicksburg campaign in Jackson, Mississippi, under Confederate General Joseph E. Johnston, Helm and his men acted as a rear guard for Johnston's men as they retreated.

Helm and his men then set up camp on July 21, 1863, at a place near Morton, which the soldiers affectionately called "Camp Hurricane." Writing to his wife, Helm related the poor conditions at the camp: "We have to drink water that, in ordinary times, you wouldn't offer your horse; and I have hardly slept out of a swamp since we left Jackson."

After about thirty days, the brigade was quickly transported to Chattanooga, arriving on September 3rd, to help Bragg, who had his hands full with the fast approaching Union General William S. Rosecrans in what one historian calls "the culmination of a month long game of cat and mouse between Rosecrans' Federal Army of the Cumberland and Bragg's Confederate Army of Tennessee."

Particularly galling to Bragg was that prior to the outbreak of the battle itself a number of his own generals ignored his direct orders, including Confederate luminaries like General Leonidas Polk, who demanded more troops.

Yet with a third plan in his mind, and after cajoling his commanders into action, Bragg finally ordered a full attack at about two o'clock on Saturday, September 19th that resumed in full at 9:45 on the next morning near a creek called Chickamauga, the Cherokee Indian word for "River of Death."

Helm's Brigade launched three blistering and bloody attacks on Union General George H. Thomas' troops at the far right side of a six-mile long line. Yet Thomas' line held, earning him the sobriquet "The Rock of Chickamauga."

But that was about all of the bright news for the Union, for many historians call the battle "the most complete defeat suffered by the Union Army during the Civil War," and most assuredly a stunning blow to the Federals' efforts in the West.

The Union suffered 16,179 casualties, while the Grays lost even more, about 18,500 casualties, one of the bloodiest days of the entire war. In the words of Confederate General D.H. Hill, it was a "hollow victory."

Private John Jackson of the "Orphan Brigade," describes another part of the action those two days when Helm and his men were caught in what McMurtry called a "withering crossfire":

About 10:00 a.m. Major Wilson rode up to General Helm, who was sitting against a tree in [the] rear of our regiment talking to Colonel C. and gave him the verbal order from Breckinridge to advance in fifteen minutes and adjust his movements on the right. The general got up and mounted his horse, laughing and talking as on parade.

Suddenly, Helm was struck in the right side with a musket ball and fell from his horse, mortally wounded. Carried from the field by two of his lieutenants, Helm lingered until evening. His last word was a triumphant "Victory!" Today, a marker at the battlefield designates the spot where he fell.

For the sixteenth President, Chickamauga was a double blow: there was the bitter defeat, and next he had lost a favorite brother-in-law.

Lincoln, upon hearing of Helm's death is reported to have said in his grief, "I feel as David of old did when he was told of the death of Absalom."

Tragically, Helm was only thirty-two years old when he died. The flourishing law practice was gone, the devoted marriage was gone, and his fledgling career in politics was gone. It was all over for this young, bright, promising Kentuckian: a life snuffed out before its time near the bloody creek called Chickamauga.

Kentuckian Emilie Todd Helm: "Little Sister" Causes a Stir at the White House

Recently, more Civil War historians are focusing on the impact of the conflict on those who stayed at home. While not discounting the sheer terror and raw violence of the battles and skirmishes, these chroniclers of war wonder what effect the conflict had on various people back home: the elderly, and the children, and the widows of fallen soldiers.

But what if the grieving widow of a Confederate general was the sister-in-law of the Commander-in-Chief of the opponent's army?

What if in her grief that same Confederate widow sought condolence from her favorite sister, who just happened to live in the White House?

And how would the President of the United States react when the widow was firmly convinced that her husband had died for a just and noble cause, one completely at odds with the President's?

Indeed, that was the situation in the late fall of 1863, when Emilie Todd Helm, Mary Todd Lincoln's half sister, requested permission to visit the White House after the death of Emile's husband, Kentucky Confederate General Ben Hardin Helm at the Battle of Chickamauga. Mrs. Helm was convinced that the succor she sought from Mary would help to allay the deep sense of loss the younger Todd felt. In truth, older Mary was like a mother to the attractive young widow.

Fortunately, Emilie Helm left a fairly detailed record of her visit to the executive mansion in a series of letters recorded by her niece Katherine Helm in *Mary, Wife of Lincoln*.

What happened to get Emilie to the White House and what happened after she arrived have been parts of a little noted chapter in the life of President and Mrs. Lincoln. It is a story that not only says something about the effect of the ravages of war on the home folks, but in turn reveals the kindness and patience of the sixteenth President, who was torn surely by the conflicting questions of the obligations he had to the nation and those he had to the family of his wife.

Adding to all this difficulty was the grief Lincoln himself felt when he learned of his brother-in-law's death. Lincoln was quite fond of General Helm, even offering him a position as paymaster for the Union army at the outbreak of the war.

Emilie Todd Helm: "Little Sister" to Lincoln and Mary Lincoln's sister. Courtesy of the Kentucky Historical Society.

But Helm cast his lot with the Confederacy and quickly rose to the rank of general, heading for a brief time, the famous First Kentucky Brigade, known as the "Orphan Brigade," that potent and dedicated fighting force that seemed to never give up in spite of overwhelming odds.

When Lincoln learned of Helm's death at Chickamauga on September 20, 1863, he is reported as saying, "I feel as David did of old when he was told of the death of Absalom. 'Would to God that I had died for thee! Oh, Absalom, my son, my son.'" A contemporary of Lincoln, Senator David Davis, said he "never saw Mr. Lincoln more moved" than he was after learning of Helm's death.

And he was just as fond of Emilie, affectionately calling her "Little Sister," expressing a kind of paternal affection toward his young, distraught sister-in-law with a cherubic face and flashing and expressive eyes. Lincoln had grown fond of her after an extended visit to the Lincoln's Springfield, Illinois home during Emilie's late adolescence.

Yet the situation was slippery. Emilie Helm had made it quite clear where her sympathies lay: she bled Confederate gray in every sense of the phrase; there wasn't any doubt about that. To make matters worse, the swirling rumors around Washington had it that Mary was in actuality a Confederate spy, an accusation certainly totally unfounded. But Mary's four brothers' fighting for the Confederacy and three sisters' being married to Confederate soldiers did not help allay any fears in Washington in spite of Mrs. Lincoln's firm and unwavering dedication to the Union cause. Emilie Helm's visit to the White House would stoke the fires of rumor surrounding the First Lady.

The first problem, though, was getting Emile Helm across Union lines and to the White House.

Emilie Helm, living in Selma, Alabama at the time, enlisted the help of Confederate General Braxton Bragg who asked Union General U.S. Grant to allow her to cross the lines and make her way back to Lexington, Kentucky to be consoled by her mother, Betsy Todd.

But Grant refused the pleadings of the grieving widow and her benefactors, until Lincoln himself interceded, sending a note telling anyone questioning her that he authorized her to "have protection of person and property" to return to Kentucky as she had planned. But she ultimately made it to Fort Monroe, Virginia, where she was refused permission to cross the lines because she would not sign an oath of allegiance to the United States. In her mind, to swear allegiance to the United States would demean her beloved husband's memory.

The soldiers who dealt with her reasoned that even the sister-in-law of the President had to swear allegiance, but, of course, Emilie Helm stood firm in her decision, displaying a bit of that Todd stubbornness her sister Mary was so famous for.

Finally, one of the Union officers decided to break the impasse and to telegraph the President, who promptly sent a short, curt reply: "Send her to me."

In spite of her intransigence, Mrs. Emilie Todd Helm was greeted graciously by both of the Lincolns. Emilie Helm wrote later that "Mr. Lincoln and my sister met me with the warmest affection; we were all too grief-stricken at first for speech. I had lost my husband, they had lost their fine little son Willie, and Mary and I had lost three brothers in the Confederate service. We could only embrace each other in silence and tears."

As might be expected, the awkwardness of the situation tainted the atmosphere of the sisters' relationship and conversation. Emilie Helm observed that "allusion to the present is like tearing open a fresh and bleeding wound and the pain is too great for self-control.

And the future, alas, the future is empty of everything but despair." She continues, "This frightful war comes between us like a barrier of granite, closing our lips but not our hearts."

But having Emilie there was comforting to the President, too, who took Emilie Helm aside long enough to confide in her that he was "worried about Mary, her nerves have gone to pieces; she cannot hide from me the strain she has been under has been too much for her mental as well as her physical health." The President, it seemed, thought that this visit from Emilie would also help Mary regain her equilibrium after the death of her son Willie and after her extended bereavement.

One of the ways was for Emilie to be a sounding board for Mary, who one day in utter frustration held out her arms to Emilie and cried, "Kiss me, Emilie, and tell me that you love me! I seem to be the scapegoat for both the North and South!"

However bad things got, they got considerably worse when General Dan Sickles and Senator Ira Harris visited the White House.

In the course of what had to be a strained conversation, General Sickles, who had recently sacrificed one of his legs at the Battle of Gettysburg, told Lincoln, referring to Emilie Helm, that "You should not have that rebel in your house!"

Lincoln came through with one for the family: "Excuse me, General Sickles, my wife and I are in the habit of choosing our own guests. We do not need from our friends either advice or assistance in that matter."

Then, it was Senator Harris' turn. He directed Emilie Helm: "Well," he began, "We have whipped the rebels at Chattanooga and I hear, madam, that the scoundrels ran like scared rabbits."

Emilie promptly replied: "It was the example, Senator Harris, that you set them at Bull Run and Manassas!"

Then, the senator broached a subject quite tender to Mary Lincoln, her son Robert's serving in the Union Army.

"Why isn't Robert in the Army? He is old enough and strong enough to serve his country. He should have gone to the front some time ago."

Ms. Helm records that at that moment, "Sister Mary's face turned white as death," having already suffered the terrible loss of two of her children.

Mary replied that Robert, at the time a college student at Harvard, "was no shirker. If fault there be, it is mine. I have insisted that he should stay in college a little longer, as I think an educated man can serve his country with more intelligent purpose than an ignoramus."

But Harris wouldn't let go and turned and addressed Emilie Helm: "Madam, if I had twenty sons they should all be fighting the rebels."

Mrs. Helm couldn't hold her tongue. "And if I had twenty sons, Senator Harris, they should be opposing yours!"

Even the children mirrored the tension. One day, Lincoln's son, Tad, and Emilie Helm's daughter, Katherine, engaged in a spirited conversation when Tad was showing his young cousin pictures from a photograph album. Tad pointed at his father's picture and announced, "This is the President!"

Katherine's reply was: "No, that is not the President. Mr. Davis is President."

"Hurrah for Abe Lincoln!" Tad shouted.

"Hurrah for Jeff Davis!" Katherine answered.

Tad went running to his father to settle the argument. Lincoln put both children on his lap and said: "Well, Tad, you know who is your President, and I am your little cousin's Uncle Lincoln."

Soon the awkwardness of Confederate sympathizers holed up in the White House got to be too much. Emilie realized it and probably the Lincolns did, too. Lincoln asked her again to sign an oath of allegiance. But again she refused.

But Emilie decided to use the pass that Lincoln had given her and make her way back to Lexington to visit her mother.

Later, Lincoln heard reports that back in Kentucky General Stephen Burbridge had wanted to arrest Emilie Helm, but wouldn't because of who she was and Lincoln's pass.

Lincoln wrote General Burbridge a note about Ms. Helm: "I do not intend to protect her against the consequences of disloyal words or acts spoken or done by her since her return to Kentucky. Deal with her for current conduct, just as you would with any other."

The tension between her and the President grew even more pronounced when Emilie, in the fall of 1864, demanded that she be allowed to sell 600 bales of her Alabama cotton to raise much needed cash for living expenses. While Lincoln could have authorized such a sale, he refused on the grounds that she had not sworn an allegiance to the Union, and, therefore was a party to the enemy.

Emilie left in a huff.

Back in Lexington, she composed a scathing letter about her and her family's destitution that she addressed to "Mr. Lincoln," reminding him that it was his "minie bullets have made us what we are."

Jean Baker's biography of Mary Todd Lincoln says that Emilie's remarks were words "her half sister never forgave."

Thus, the ravages of war don't just affect the soldiers in the field. They have consequences even for the widows and children. The Emilie Todd Helm visits to the White House help us vividly understand how the long arm of destruction can have some unpredictable consequences. But, perhaps, more importantly, that President Lincoln permitted a Rebel to visit the executive mansion during the Civil War also says something quite redeeming about a man of great burdens who had a measure of compassion even for his enemies.

General Humphrey Marshall: A Little Too Political to be Military

As a military leader, Kentuckian General Humphrey Marshall was not very impressive. During the Civil War he won few battles, none terribly significant. But he is important to Kentucky Civil War history because he symbolizes the heavy political aspects of the war in the Bluegrass State, aspects that affected the course of events for the Confederacy–and the state itself.

In *Battle Tactics of the Civil War*, the widely respected military historian Paddy Griffith notes that during the war, "the personality clashes, intrigues, and unjust policies of so many Civil War officers doomed them to fall far short of the absolute standards of efficiency which might have been attained...." Such is a good description of Marshall.

In particular, Marshall was both a trained soldier with military experience in Mexico and an active politician prior to the war and certainly during it.

Born January 13, 1812, in Frankfort, Kentucky, he was a relative of Chief Justice John Marshall, and, curiously, a nephew of James G. Birney, an important anti-slavery leader.

Marshall graduated forty-second in a class of forty-five in 1832 from the United States Military Academy. But he quickly tired of the military life and resigned his commission in 1833 to study law, starting his career in Louisville, while also devoting time to agriculture in nearby Henry County. He was admitted to the bar in 1833.

After fighting in the Black Hawk War in Illinois (the same war that Abraham Lincoln served in), he began what was a life-long interest in politics when he was elected to the Louisville City Council and became active in the state militia, rising to the rank of lieutenant colonel by 1846.

At the outbreak of the Mexican War, he assumed the rank of colonel of the First Kentucky Calvary, distinguishing himself at the Battle of Buena Vista in February of 1847.

With a solid military experience behind him, Marshall was elected to the House of Representatives in 1849 and served President Millard Fillmore faithfully, who appointed him minister to China from 1852 to 1853.

Upon his return to the United States, he was elected to the House again in 1855 on the American Party ticket, defeating William Preston, later to be General William Preston, C.S.A.

One of his soldiers, Edward O. Guerrant, notes that Marshall often boasted of his political victories over nationally known figures like Joe Lecomte, and Kentuckians like Joseph Holt and Cassius Clay—"victories over all," Marshall said.

He quickly gained a reputation as a secessionist, but worked diligently to keep Kentucky in the Union as a neutral state.

Yet he vehemently opposed Lincoln when Lincoln sent troops into Kentucky to secure the state for the Union.

Marshall then joined the Confederate Army and was given the rank of brigadier general on October 30, 1861, and assigned command of the Army of Southwest Virginia, a post he soon grew to hate, pestering the beleaguered Confederate government for a different assignment. According to Marshall, President Davis himself promised Marshall personally enough troops to "liberate" Kentucky, a promise that either Davis didn't make or failed to fulfill.

Two historians, William C. Davis and Meredith Swentor, call Marshall "no easy taskmaster. Alternately lazy and energetic, forgetful, disorganized, forever carping at the War Department and his fellow generals, he may been unfailingly interesting, but he was frequently exasperating."

Marshall is best known as the commander of Confederate forces at the Battle of Middle Creek, the most significant battle in Eastern Kentucky, fought in Floyd County on January 10, 1862.

His opponent was Colonel James A. Garfield, later president of the United States.

Because Garfield forced Marshall and his army back to Southwest Virginia, the battle made national headlines because the Union was in desperate need of a victory of any sort after so many defeats in the Eastern Theater.

One historian adds that the battle was also significant because it symbolized the "fratricidal, neighbor-against-neighbor warfare that characterized the struggle for Kentucky," with men from both sides with deep Kentucky roots, who engaged in fierce "hand to hand combat" in the struggle to control Eastern Kentucky.

Finally, the battle also called in question Marshall's ability as a military leader when he and his forces fell for a ruse that revealed his position and led to a Union victory. It worked this way: Garfield ordered a dash into the valley to draw fire from Marshall's forces and reveal their position above the valley, although the Union troops sustained heavy fire and drove the Confederates up the hill.

Marshall, fearing his men would desert him, retreated, burning his wagons and supplies as he and his troops retreated.

Marshall's effectiveness as a general soon became a topic of conversation among his superiors in Richmond, as the powers there began to doubt his abilities as a military leader, while Marshall continued to badger Richmond for another assignment.

Part of Marshall's ineffectiveness was due to his lax discipline. It was so bad that one soldier even quipped that he "would eat the first man the general should shoot for any crime."

Whatever the estimation of Marshall as a military leader, at the same time, he continued to politic to secure another command somewhere else, an idea, in view of Marshall's lack of success, that must have seemed ludicrous to his superiors.

In March, two months later, Marshall was ordered to fall back to Pound Gap, another important entry point through the mountains into Kentucky.

Complaining to Richmond about his supply routes and the lack of food, Marshall reluctantly obeyed, for his superiors hoped to slow the progress of any advance by the Union army.

A correspondent from the *Cincinnati Gazette* described the march to the gap by Garfield's men as "following the creeks and rivulets, the constant rain and snow soaking both officers and men to the skin, and the bottomless, endless mud formed a combination of untoward circumstances, difficult to overcome."

Garfield knew that the enemy was deeply entrenched on the crest of the mountain, yet he had a plan he described later in an article in the *North American Review* for December of 1886.

He said he sent "his cavalry around by the regular road, and at a given hour attacked the enemy's pickets, driving them in, and making a demonstration upon their contact to attract their attention." Then he sent his infantry up the mountain, "when the ascent was precipitous" to "attack the enemy in flank and rear." The enemy was then distracted by the cavalry and gave the Union soldiers their full attention, not noticing that they were soon to be attacked from the rear and the flank.

General Humphrey Marshall: Large in size, but built for politics, not war. Courtesy of the Kentucky Historical Society.

Garfield concludes that "in a fight of less than twenty minutes' duration, they were utterly routed."

Garfield then occupied the enemy camp of sixty log-houses, which he and his men later burned.

Once again, a trained military man had been outsmarted by a lowly college professor from northern Ohio–hardly pleasing Marshall's commanders back in Richmond.

After again requesting an assignment out of the mountains, and being turned down, Marshall, who had had some success for a change at Princeton, West Virginia, resigned in a huff on June 16, 1862.

But the Confederacy, planning an invasion of Kentucky in the fall, needed as many prominent Kentuckians as possible, and Marshall was reappointed to his position three days later.

The Confederacy's plan was to invade the state from several entry points. General Braxton Bragg would start from middle Tennessee, General Kirby Smith would enter from Cumberland Gap and General Marshall would enter the Bluegrass from the east.

But, of course, the Battle of Perryville proved to be too much for Bragg, and Marshall and his forces, finally making it just to Mount Sterling, would only serve as a possible defense of Bragg's retreating forces from the area, which, in the end, never materialized.

As one biographer notes, Bragg and Marshall did not "connect"—in more ways than one.

Bragg's biographer, Grady McWhiney, notes that Bragg wrote that Marshall was "a great humbug and superficial, though a fool." Bragg even questioned Marshall's leadership in the war in Mexico, noting that Marshall's "regiment did some fine running and no fighting, as all mounted volunteers ever will do."

At any rate, his superiors did not ask him to re-consider when Marshall again resigned on June 17, 1863. With his poor military record, one biographer noted that "nobody tried to dissuade him."

Marshall made his way to Richmond, Virginia to open a law office. But the lure of politics was too great, and he was elected a member of the Kentucky delegation, serving from May 2, 1864 to March 18, 1865.

According to one biographer, while a representative, he served as a member of the Military Affairs Committee and soon became a thorn in the side of President Jefferson Davis and Braxton Bragg, opposing them on practically every military measure, including many tax bills and the suspension of the writ of habeas corpus.

But he had not forgotten his native state, and ceaselessly lobbied for another invasion of Kentucky, plying his political tools on a hopeless set of circumstances, a dream never to be realized.

When the Confederacy fell, Marshall fled to Mexico and then to Texas and Louisiana, but returned to Kentucky in 1866 and again practiced law until he died on March 28, 1872.

Marshall was a large man, weighing in at over 300 pounds. He believed in spiritualism, a fact noted by Edward O. Guerrant who described a séance where Marshall's daughter, Ella, served as the medium, while his mother was the spirit.

At any rate, Marshall never realized his potential as a military leader, and never became the politician he sought to be. Davis and Swentor conclude that Marshall "was stuck in a backwater, with no military action, experiencing the war vicariously from afar through newspapers and wildly fantastic rumors."

But he became a symbol of the frustration of politics that were so much a part of the Civil War in the South and the frustration, ultimately, of a lost cause.

Englishman George St. Leger Grenfell: General John Hunt Morgan's Military Man

Besides the general himself, the cast of characters for General John Hunt Morgan's Confederate 2nd Kentucky Cavalry rivals almost any from a playwright's imagination. It includes Champ Ferguson, who never met a Yankee he didn't want to kill; George "Lightning" Ellsworth, whose antics with the telegraph kept many soldiers in blue and their friends utterly confused or totally baffled; Captain Thomas Hines, whose skill at organizing clandestine activities and prison escapes outdid almost anyone in the Confederacy; and Jerome Clarke, known as "Sue Mundy" who, as a "lady guerrilla" late in war, seemed to be everywhere at once.

But one more character needs to be on the playbill who wasn't even an American, a soldier whose valuable advice and military experience served Morgan and his men well on several crucial occasions.

He was an Englishman in his late fifties after all, a time when most men put away foolish notions about the grandeur of war, a soldier of fortune, a man who fought in various wars just for the thrill of it, and a man with an imposing British name, George St. Leger Grenfell, "St. Lege" to his men.

It is difficult to overestimate his importance to Morgan and his men, for even though his stay with Morgan was only about eight months, by word and by example Colonel Grenfell brought a stiff dose of discipline to the "alligator soldiers" who were then hardly shining examples of military decorum.

Before he joined Morgan, Grenfell had a world of colorful experience fighting around the world. According to the reminiscences of General Basil Duke, Morgan's second in command, Grenfell served in the French cavalry in Algeria, fought in Morocco, India, the Crimean War, and South America, anywhere he was given, according to Duke, "every opportunity to gratify his rather extraordinary appetite for hazardous adventure."

So, hearing about the Civil War in the United States, Grenfell couldn't resist the temptation to serve on the side of the Confederacy. So he brought letters of introduction to General Robert E. Lee. Lee, in turn, felt that Grenfell could best serve the South by aligning himself with General John Hunt Morgan, reasoning, as Duke relates, that it was "utterly impossible for him to deny himself an excellent opportunity for occupation and excitement in his favourite vocation...." Morgan took to him quickly and Grenfell soon became Morgan's adjutant general.

Many of Grenfell's biographers describe him as a character ripped from the pages of a Sir Walter Scott novel like *Ivanhoe*, for he bore all the earmarks of a gallant gladiator in appearance and demeanor. Duke characterizes him as "tall, erect, and of military bearing. His frame was spare, but sinewy and athletic, and he preserved the activity of youth. His bold, aquiline features were scorched by the Eastern sun to a swarthy hue, and his face, while handsome, wore always a defiant, and sometimes fierce expression." He had an air of nobility about him, a refined, yet a curiously rugged demeanor that commanded and got immediate respect, even possessing, what Duke colorfully called "reckless eccentricity."

To illustrate, after a battle in a campaign commanded by Confederate General Braxton Bragg, Grenfell suffered from an infected finger on his left hand. He tried to get surgeons to amputate the finger, but they all refused. Angry and impatient, Grenfell took matters in his own hands by placing the digit on a wooden block and proceeding to chop off the offending finger.

Another time, he and Ellsworth clashed near Crab Orchard, Kentucky. It seemed Ellsworth was highly irritated by a bushwhacker who continued to fire into the column of men as they rode along the way. Impulsively, Ellsworth grabbed a horse, Grenfell's special horse, without his permission, and dashed toward the offending party. But the bushwhacker was too good of a shot, and in the fray Ellsworth lost not only Grenfell's fine steed, but also the Britisher's English saddle, and a coat containing all of Grenfell's gold money. When Ellsworth returned sans horse and saddle and money, one biographer describes

Grenfell as "an excited volcano [who] sought to slay [Ellsworth] instantly." It took three days before Grenfell simmered down enough to be in Ellsworth's company.

But when the colonel roared into battle, his anger and stealth focused keenly on the enemy. On July 17, 1862, the Englishman showed his stuff at the Battle of Cynthiana, Kentucky. There Grenfell charged the railroad depot where many of the enemy were holed up. In a mad dash, Grenfell took eleven bullets through his horse, person, and clothes—including a shot through his signature scarlet skullcap—and still came out of the fracas with only minor injuries.

Yet Cynthiana wasn't the only place where Grenfell demonstrated his bravery. At Tompkinsville, Kentucky, during Morgan's July raid, part of Morgan's men were pressing on the left and right, with another group coming up behind the enemy, when, all of a sudden, Grenfell dug his spurs into his horse's side and charged madly up the middle, leaped a fence where the enemy was hiding, and slashed at them wildly with his saber. Amazingly, all of this action came from a man approaching sixty years old.

But while he could lead by example, that wasn't really the reason Lee sent Grenfell to Morgan. Morgan's reputation in Richmond was that although he and his men didn't lack bravery, they were as a whole quite an undisciplined group. Individual soldiers often left the group to visit family and friends, wandering the countryside, looking for food and horses, and generally not bearing the cache of the military demeanor so important to success in war.

Grenfell saw as his job to whip this group of Rebels into line. Indeed, Morgan biographer Howard Swigget credits Grenfell for much of Morgan's success. For Grenfell brought to bear all the rich experience he had had around the world as a soldier of fortune and tried desperately to impose that discipline on Morgan's men. Swigget concludes, for example, that "it cannot be a coincidence that when Grenfell was along there was complete success and when he was absent there was disaster."

At Sparta, Tennessee, while Morgan and his men were in camp, Grenfell saw to it that there was strict discipline. From an orderly, experienced military mind, Grenfell made sure that there were guards to alert the rest of the approaching enemy. There was drill and there was parading to train the young men in the ways of war.

Yet it was this devotion to military ways that ultimately lead to a break in the relationship between Grenfell and Morgan. Morgan picked W.C.P. Breckinridge to command Morgan's Second Brigade, an appointment that angered Grenfell immensely because he wanted the position, and he had little regard for Breckinridge anyway. Grenfell insisted that Morgan pick someone else, but Morgan was firm in his decision. Angry and hurt, Grenfell quickly collected his swords and horses and left Morgan's command. Ironically, even after Grenfell's show of temper, Morgan still heaped praise on Grenfell saying that, "the service loses a fine soldier. He is certainly one of the most gallant men I ever saw."

George St. Leger Grenfell: British by birth, a professional soldier in General John Hunt Morgan's unit, known for his daring.

Morgan chronicler James Ramage concludes that Grenfell ultimately failed in his mission to impose pervasive discipline on Morgan's men because of the personality of Morgan himself. As a "gambler" and "hedonist," Morgan's style of leadership was hardly a model of military manners. Morgan even said once, "I prefer fifty men who gladly obey me to a division I have to watch and punish." Consequently, Morgan permitted himself to largely ignore military rigidity, and didn't expect his men to adhere to a strict code either—something Grenfell eventually could not abide. Grenfell summed up his estimate of Morgan and his men, quipping that he, "had never encountered such men who would fight like the devil, but would do as they pleased, like these damned Rebel cavalrymen."

Grenfell quickly joined the staff of another cavalry leader, General J.E.B. Stuart, bitterness still sticking in his craw. According to one of Morgan's biographers, Grenfell confided with Virginian Unionist, John Minor Botts, that Morgan's men were "a band of horse thieves and plunderers of public and private property, carrying on a system of warfare to which [I] had not been accustomed and which was revolting to [my] nature." Bitter words from a man who really felt that he had been slighted. But it was a wound that quickly healed.

Later in the war, Grenfell acted as an advocate for Morgan in the Confederate capital, pleading with the powers in Richmond to give Morgan more men and supplies, something Ramage described as Grenfell's "twist[ing] arms with vigor."

Eventually, Grenfell hooked up with Morgan's men one last time, Captain Thomas Hines, this time, in the ill-fated Northwest Conspiracy, an elaborate scheme to unite all the Southern supporters in the Midwest and eventually lure these states into the Confederacy.

The plan, of course, failed, but since the captured Grenfell was a foreigner, he received an unusually stiff sentence. He served his time on a small island called Dry Tortugus, a hellhole off the coast of Florida. While there, he suffered the gross indignities of torture and mutilation in spite of his humanitarian aid to those suffering in the prison from an epidemic of yellow fever with Grenfell ably assisting fellow prisoner Dr. Samuel Mudd of Lincoln's assassination infamy. Presumably, Grenfell was lost at sea when he and four of his fellow prisoners tried to escape in a raging storm and are thought to have drowned in what was Grenfell's last adventure.

The colorful character certainly brought life and tried to impose military demeanor on Morgan and his unruly men. While he was not successful, in the end, he still stands as one among a cast of players any playwright would love to have strut their hours on the stage.

"Lightning Ellsworth": Morgan's Telegraph Man

All wars produce their cast of unusual and exciting characters, men and women who seem to have uncanny abilities to produce the unexpected, to be able to do what others find impossible or improbable.

Such a man was George "Lightning" Ellsworth, General John Hunt Morgan's crack telegraph operator.

If soldiers had a typical demeanor and appearance, it certainly wasn't like that of Ellsworth. Described by Morgan biographer Dee Alexander Brown as "jaunty" with eyelids [that] drooped under a high forehead." [H]is nose was aquiline with a bump in the bridge; the expression in his eyes was disdainful, cynical, devil-may-care."

Another Morgan biographer, Howard Swiggett, described Ellsworth as having "the tragic mask of the great comedian." Photographs taken of Ellsworth in his later years confirm that even as a old man, he still retained that comic face that seemed always to incite laughter and frivolity.

How Ellsworth ended up in Morgan's command is equally fascinating. Born in Canada, as a young man Ellsworth was enthralled by the telegraph. Accordingly, he moved to Washington, D.C., where he graduated from Samuel Morse's telegraph school. Ellsworth then took a job in Kentucky as a telegraph operator and met Morgan in Lexington. In 1860, Ellsworth moved to Houston, but shortly after the war broke out, Morgan remembered Ellsworth and what he could do and sent for him.

For Morgan recalled that Ellsworth had a number of talents with the telegraph. According to Brown, Ellsworth could "read rapid-fire code, imitate other telegraphers, and was familiar with the sending styles of many operators who were working for the federal in Kentucky and Tennessee."

Ellsworth possessed a pocket-sized instrument that allowed him to tap into a line without interrupting the flow of electricity. In other words, he could both receive and send messages, a fact that allowed him to, according to Swigget, "cause havoc in Northern Headquarters."

He earned his nickname not from his ability to send code at unbelievable speeds, but from an event in Horse Cave, Kentucky, where he cut the circuit and pretended to be answering for all the towns along the line during a violent thunderstorm.

George "Lightning" Ellsworth: His bogus telegraphs drove Union commanders crazy.

In his own words, Ellsworth later said, "My situation was anything but an agreeable one, sitting in the mud, with my feet in the water up to my knees."

As one observer recalled it, one bolt "danced along the overhead wires and sparked off the key in [Ellsworth's] hand." But he persisted and soon he learned where the enemy was, where he was headed and how Morgan could proceed with the intended invasion plans.

But this wasn't the full extent of the use that Morgan made of the resourceful Ellsworth. Indeed, Ellsworth confused the enemy on so many occasions by sending bogus messages that his fame added yet another dimension to the "Morgan myth."

Once, at Midway, Ellsworth took over the keys at the telegraph office and promptly told the train conductor that there were no rebels in the area, but Ellsworth received a message from Lexington, saying that Morgan and his men <u>were</u> in Midway and the Federals were on their way from Frankfort to engage Morgan in Midway. But with Ellsworth at the key and in the Midway operator's style, Ellsworth telegraphed that Morgan and his men were not in Midway, but they were headed for Frankfort. Lexington, fearing an attack on Frankfort, called back the Union troops from Frankfort. In Frankfort's name, Ellsworth telegraphed Lexington that Morgan's troops were there. Chaos reigned: Just where were Morgan and his men?

Amid all the Confusion, Morgan and his men headed for Georgetown, where Ellsworth prevented communication between Frankfort and Lexington, while Morgan and his men rested for two days and gathered new recruits. It hardly seemed that Ellsworth could be any more bedeviling.

But he was.

One time, at Somerset, in a message signed with Morgan's name, Ellsworth bid farewell to General Jeremiah Boyle, commander of federal troops in Kentucky, with this message:

> Good morning Jerry. This telegraph is a great institution. You should destroy it as it keeps me posted too well. My friend Ellsworth has all your dispatches since July 10 on file. Do you want copies?

And if that wasn't enough, as Basil Duke, Morgan's second in command records, Ellsworth issued a mock "order" to all telegraph operators in the area:

> Headquarters, Telegraph Dept. of KY.,
> Confederate States of America
>
> General Order No. 1
>
> When an operator is positively informed that the enemy is marching on his station, he will immediately proceed to destroy the telegraphic instruments and all the material in his charge. Such instances of carelessness, as were exhibited on the part of the operators at Lebanon and Georgetown, will be severely dealt with, by order of
>
> G.A. Ellsworth
> General Telegraph Supt.
> C.S. Telegraphic Dept.

While it may be hyperbole to say that "Lightning" Ellsworth was Morgan's most valuable man, it doesn't defy credulity to say that Ellsworth was an integral part of the raider's success. Certainly, he helped Morgan confuse the enemy into chaos and allowed the daring cavalry man to escape when capture was imminent. It is a mark of keen insight that Morgan recognized the use to which he could put Ellsworth and his immense talents.

Madison County's James Bennett McCreary: From Morgan's Soldier to U.S. Senator

Stories abound about the Confederate Kentucky Second Cavalry, about its charismatic leader, Lexingtonian General John Hunt Morgan, and his colorful band of men.

There's his second in command and brother-in-law Colonel Basil Duke, whose great courage under fire and reasoned military strategies proved invaluable on numerous difficult occasions.

Or there's Thomas Hines, whose daring covert missions led the Union military to describe him as "the most dangerous man in the Confederacy."

Or there's George "Lightning" Ellsworth, Morgan's telegraph man whose ability to send bogus telegraph messages sent many Yankee soldiers scurrying in the wrong direction.

Or also include the swashbuckling British soldier of fortune, Sir Leger Grenfell, whose daring deeds and devil-may-care attitude earned the respect of friends and foes.

There's also Logan County's Marcellus Jerome Clarke, later known as "Sue Mundy," who, like fellow Morgan compadre, Clinton County's Champ Ferguson, gained notoriety as two of Kentucky's most infamous guerrillas.

Or there's Roy Cluke, too, a valuable soldier, leader of men, and an integral part of Morgan's machine, who ended up dying in a military prisoner of war camp.

Or include also the clever Adam "Stovepipe" Johnson, famous for his clever ruse in southern Indiana at Newburgh that led to the surrender of a federal arsenal.

But after the war, Kentucky's sympathies had turned decidedly southern as a result of its perception that the federal government had treated the Commonwealth unfairly.

In fact, from Governor Thomas Bramlette's alleged switch to a more southern stance during his 1863-1867 administration until 1891, all of the governors of Kentucky were either ex-Confederate soldiers or avowed southern supporters. It seemed that southern sympathies or service in the Confederate army was a necessary prerequisite for election to statewide office.

On that list was James Bennett McCreary, elected to the state's highest office twice, serving as governor from 1875-1879 and again from 1911-1915.

Besides other offices at the state level, McCreary also was elected to the U.S. House of Representatives from 1903-1909 and as U.S. senator from Kentucky from 1903-1909.

Born on July 8, 1838, the son of Dr. Edmund R. and Sabrina Bennett McCreary in Richmond, Kentucky, McCreary graduated from Centre College in Danville in 1857. There he made friends with many others who served the Stars and Bars, and then he studied law at Cumberland University in Lebanon, Tennessee until 1859, when he was admitted to the bar, and returned home to open a law office in Richmond, shortly thereafter.

While McCreary's political career has been the subject of considerable interest to state historians, not many writers have looked at his years as a Confederate soldier. Fortunately, though, McCreary left a rather extensive diary detailing many of his days in service to Morgan and the Confederacy, and his diary, along with other contemporary sources, chronicles an interesting story of bravery, gallantry, and great sacrifice for the cause he so fervently believed in.

What attracted McCreary to the Confederate cause and subsequently to service in the Rebel army was the overwhelming Union defeat and stunning Confederate victory in his hometown at the Battle of Richmond on August 29-30, 1862, that resulted in a whopping 4300 Union prisoners and over 1000 killed or wounded. While some historians argue that the battle at Chickamauga was a more one-sided Confederate victory, there is no doubt that the Battle of Richmond was a crushing and demoralizing defeat for the Union.

And the young 24 year-old McCreary quickly got caught up in the spirit of the Rebel victory.

In his journal, his ebullience is obvious: "The whole country swarms with rebel soldiers. War waves its graceful pennons over our fertile fields and once peaceful pastures and bristling bayonets, frowning cannon, and thousands of sturdy soldiers prove that the South is terribly earnest and they who sought to oppress us will be oppressed by the stench and surfeited by the blood poured by the Southern bullet, shell and sabre from the bodies of Northern hirelings."

Emboldened by such élan, now Major McCreary and others in the Richmond area raised a regiment, ultimately called the 11th Kentucky Cavalry, known as Chenault's Cavalry for its leader, Richmond native David Waller Chenault, a unit later attached to Morgan's Second Kentucky Cavalry.

But McCreary's enthusiasm for everything Confederate was not shared by his parents: "My parents are opposed to my going into the army and my politics. God knows I love them dearly and as their only son I would have remained at home…but I cannot stay in peace, and I believe it my solemn duty to assist in hurling back oppression and ruin from people of whom I am a part."

In a few weeks, on October 7th, he was witness to the installation of Richard Hawes as the Confederate Governor of Kentucky, although only for a few hours, as Union troops soon spoiled the inauguration festivities in Frankfort.

But McCreary had to vent his enthusiasm, noting that "Today, I trust, will long shine in history and be remembered in the hearts of liberty loving Kentuckians as the day of exodus from abolition and tyranny."

Yet just a few days later, although he describes himself as "a listener and looker-on," he was a participant in the somewhat indecisive, but bloody battle at Perryville on October 8, 1862, described by Civil War historian Kenneth Noe as "the grand havoc of battle," and termed by others as "The Battle for Kentucky."

It was a frustrating time for McCreary. As the Confederates began their retreat from The Bluegrass State, largely unable to arouse its people to the Southern cause, his enthusiasm now was quite muted: "The cherished hopes and bright prospects so gloriously ushered in but two days since are fading, floating swiftly away."

Interestingly, during the long march back south, McCreary was asked to confiscate cattle to feed the many men in Bragg's hungry army. But since he was near Kingston in Madison County, McCreary refused, and explained his reasoning: "Not wishing to make any depredations in my own county, I left camp and turned the command over to the next officer." It was, indeed, a loyalty to place that he displayed on more than just one occasion.

Slowly, his regiment made their way south, through London, Barbourville, and on through Cumberland Gap, with McCreary observing when he saw the historic opening in the mountains that "nature and art seemingly have exhausted every resource to make this an impregnable position," a conclusion full well borne out through the rest of the war.

But as he realized he was leaving his beloved Kentucky, McCreary was struck with homesickness: "Dear loved ones at home occupied my warmest feelings and I lingered behind my command to take a...farewell look at dear old Kentucky and indulge in those sweet reminiscences and dear hopes which only a soldier can appreciate."

From there, the group headed generally west through the mountains and into central Tennessee, often distracted by the dangers along the way, for not all of the local residents all of the time backed the Confederacy. On November 10th, he noted, for example, that "I have a long ride and tedious march before me through a mountain region infested with bushwhackers. I don't know whether I look forward with pleasure or regret to this tedious mission." Commonly called "Turkey Daves," bushwhackers were an integral part of the war in the mountains, men and even young boys, armed often with just squirrel guns, who might switch their loyalties like a change of clothes, often made the life of regular soldiers, both Union and Confederate, extremely perilous. Later, he passed through Lebanon, Tennessee, the home of his alma mater, Cumberland University, where he was valedictorian of his law class, and where the 11th met up with and joined John Hunt Morgan and his men.

Flooded with memories of his days in Lebanon, McCreary fondly remembered not only some of his professors and classmates, and the good times there, but also a young woman named Mattie who seems to have been the object of McCreary's affection and yet who lay buried nearby, apparently the victim of typhoid fever. A bit maudlin, yet with a sentimentality perfectly acceptable for that day, he concludes, "Much could I write here, of your peerless beauty and goodness, but I must not. In Heaven may you realize that our loss is your eternal gain."

Onto Murfreesboro, then to Sparta and McMinnville; all along the way, he commented on the beauty of the land and the loveliness of the ladies, spouting Latin phrases when English wouldn't do.

Now, December 7th, McCreary was near Hartsville, Tennessee, the scene of a tussle when Confederate forces, led by John Hunt Morgan, in the early morning, surprised Union forces under Colonel Absalom Moore at a major supply point for Union General William S. Rosecrans' forces in Nashville. While Morgan lost 149, he captured 1844 Union men and numerous wagon loads of supplies headed for Rosecrans and his men.

It was a thrilling victory for Morgan and his men. In fact, the Confederate government so appreciated what Morgan had done that he was shortly promoted to brigadier general.

McCreary was certainly in the fray, describing his part of the battle this way: "We charged the Yankees at the very outset, drove them from their heights and breastwork, and, after a fight, very hot and very severe, of nearly two hours, Moore surrendered his whole force."

McCreary couldn't help but boast: "This has been pronounced by military men the grandest achievement of the war," gushing with pride and bravado.

Soon, after a few days of rest, drill, and training, McCreary and his unit became a part of Morgan's famous Christmas Raid into Kentucky, where they were to destroy railroad lines and trestles, disrupt supply lines to Union forces in Nashville, and generally create chaos with any Union installations in the Commonwealth.

So when on December 23rd McCreary camped on Kentucky soil, he responded by recording that "it fills my heart with joy and pride that I am once more on native heather."

Gradually, Morgan and his men made their way north until they finally captured Elizabethtown, some forty-five miles south of Louisville, and then reached Muldraugh's Hill, on December 28th, where they destroyed a vital railroad trestle and stockade. The unit then headed for Boston and Bardstown, where McCreary got his first taste of command. But while other of Morgan's men took "tea with friends," he sat "before my campfire mad, hungry, sleepy, and smoking while I relieve myself by writing it down."

By the time Morgan reached Springfield, on December 30th, McCreary again commanded forces, only this time in battle as he and his men drove Union pickets back for two miles in what McCreary described as "continual fighting." As a feint, McCreary then built a number of campfires that alerted the Yankees that Rebels were in the area. After a number of sharp exchanges, McCreary rapidly retreated and caught up with Morgan, again acting as a rear guard. Amid some confusion, the broken line of men and materiel was later reunited with Morgan's main command.

Slowly, they made their way south. McCreary boasted in his journal that his rear guard had "burnt two very large pens of U.S. corn, a bridge across Green River, burnt the Green River Stockade, which was a tough job; cleaned rebels from Columbia." But he closed his journal entry for this first day of 1863 on a more reflective note : "So diary I bid you farewell, wondering what is in the great womb of the year 1863 for me. Bloody scenes and black, sunny skies and smiles will mingle, will mingle, mingle."

James McCreary: Buried in a Richmond cemetery along with Polly, his pet bird. Courtesy of the Kentucky Historical Society.

By January 6th, Confederate General Braxton Bragg ordered Morgan to fall back from his position in middle Tennessee to Tullahoma in the south-central part of The Volunteer State, prompting McCreary, after his experiences with Bragg at Perryville, to comment that "Bragg's talent seems to be all on the retreat," a sentiment shared by many contemporaries and historians of the era.

As well might be expected, McCreary was again assigned rear guard duty as Bragg and his forces fell back toward Tullahoma, but McCreary didn't agree with the strategy, commenting that "all persons regret that Bragg fell back."

In a confusing entry for January 14th, McCreary notes that rather than serve under "the old cuss, Buford, ... we have determined not to obey the order, and to avoid it, we have been ordered to Albany, Kentucky. We start early in the morning, and Col. Chenault starts immediately for Richmond to have the order changed."

So, gradually McCreary and his soldiers of Chenault's Cavalry again make their way north to Kentucky. Whether the regiment was directly disobeying an order, or whether they were given choices is not clear, but the consequence was certain: Chenault's Cavalry headed toward The Bluegrass State.

A week later, after a difficult crossing of the icy Obie River in Tennessee, when men lost valuable guns and blankets to the swirling stream, and when all suffered from the cold, wet conditions, all in the dark, McCreary and his men, after a frightening crossing, made it to shore and ultimately to the warm cabin of a local family.

There, McCreary, with time to gather his thoughts, demonstrates his considerable ability to turn a phrase: "In the presence of a lovely and amiable young lady of the house and before a warm fire I have soon forgotten the terrors of this terrible trip. How many of the noblest, best, and most beautiful of the female sex like this good creature to whom I have been talking, grow up in the wild valleys of the country unknown, unhonored, and unsung?"

By the next day, January 22, 1863, McCreary was in Albany, Kentucky, observing that "Albany was once a flourishing town of 500 inhabitants..., but it is now entirely deserted. I felt sad and sick at heart to notice the ravages of war. Storehouses, hotels, churches, lawyers' offices, dwelling houses, and court house unoccupied, and going to decay. Where once was happiness and prosperity, with busy, bustling trade, an accursed war, inaugurated to subjugate and rob the noblest people of the world...." It was a theme that he often repeated in still other cities of the state.

Until mid-June, McCreary and his fellow soldiers of Chenault's Cavalry fought a number of skirmishes in southern Kentucky and the surrounding areas, including Monticello, Burkesville, and Somerset until finally returning to camp in Tennessee. Most of these forays were relatively minor in the overall picture, but they, like many others in Kentucky during this time, were a part of the everyday life of the state.

On May 2nd, for example, McCreary noted the often ironic nature of these skirmishes as Yankees and Rebels fight over the same ground over and over. McCreary says that in Monticello, for example, the home of a young lady named Miss Inan Phillips became the shelter from which the Yankees were now shooting at him. He says, "This is a strange life. The house, where in pleasing dalliance I had spent many happy hours and where I had reason to believe that those who like me lived, became the rampart, behind which those seeking my life fight."

Once in a while, McCreary's unit would lose a soldier in battle, but just as frequently, they would lose a comrade to disease. McCreary, for instance, comments on March 1st, that "a very fatal disease, called brain fever, is prevailing in our camp. Two deaths already." Disease, as a killer of men, was not only a problem of Kentucky, but death from illnesses as innocuous as measles was a problem on all fronts of the war.

Unable to get it out of his mind, in his journal McCreary often returned to the theme of the destructiveness of war: "We bivouac in the road near Alexandria. We are now in a country once fertile and rich, but now desolated and barren by the cruel hand of war."

By June 23rd, now back in camp, McCreary learned of plans to move back into Kentucky as part of Morgan's force to be a part of what has come to be called Morgan's Great Raid. McCreary could hardly contain his excitement: "For many weeks the intended raid to Kentucky has been much talked of. Now it is a certainty. With throbbing hearts and sweet prospects of home and loved ones there, we will soon be on our dangerous but, I trust, successful trip."

Crossing into Kentucky at Burkesville, and making their way through Columbia, Morgan's forces met their first significant action at Tebbs Bend, near Campbellsville. His later analysis of the battle is pointed and objective, but his frustration and grief are obvious: "The enemy's position was impregnable and artillery could not be used. We assaulted and carried their outer works and then an abatis of trees, but many of our best men were killed or wounded."

Rather than cross the Green River there, Morgan tried another place, but, as McCreary says, "Here fell Col. Chenault" and a number of other officers in the regiment, a significant blow to the leadership of the troops themselves.

McCreary writes: "It was a sad, sorrowful day, and more tears of grief rolled over my weather-beaten cheeks on this mournful occasion than have before in years. The commencement of this raid is ominous."

Yet, despite the losses, 70 killed or wounded, and with McCreary now in command of Chenault's Regiment, Morgan and his men moved onto Newmarket, Lebanon, Springfield and Bardstown, all of the time appearing to head toward Louisville.

The Derby City, indeed, much of Kentucky, panicked, fueled by wild rumors about the size of Morgan's force and where he was headed. Estimates ran as high as 10,000 Morgan soldiers.

But rather than move toward Louisville with his main force, Morgan drifted downstream forty miles and camped on the night of July 7th in Garnettsville, a small mill town, just a few miles from Brandenburg on the Ohio River, Morgan's intended crossing point and a busy steamboat stop.

Close behind Morgan was Union General, and Greensburg native, Edward Hobson and the Second Brigade of General Henry M. Judah's 3rd Division, Department of the Ohio, scrambling to catch the elusive Morgan.

Thomas Hines and other members of Morgan's scouting party had done their job well in Brandenburg, and soon Morgan's troops had captured two steamboats, the *Alice Dean* and the *John T. McCombs*, The slow process of ferrying of horses and men into Indiana began, with the Union boat, the *Springfield*, and later the *Elk* creating as much resistance as they could, despite the Rebel's parrot guns that set them racing upriver in retreat.

Once again, McCreary was charged with the rear guard duties of protecting Morgan's men and horses as they crossed the Ohio River.

On July 9th, with Hobson's advance party close behind, McCreary described the dangerous situation in Brandenburg this way: "This morning I am left with half of the Regiment one mile from the river as a rear guard, and at daylight the Yankees moved down upon me. It was a critical and trying moment. By the interposition of Divine Providence, a heavy fog suddenly, and whilst hot skirmishing was going on, enveloped friends and foes, and the Yankees halted. Under this fog I crossed my command over the river."

As the Rebels made their way east and north in "Yankeeland," McCreary commented on what he saw. At one point, he noted that southern Indiana and Ohio were in a wild alarm: "The Governors of Indiana and Ohio have ordered out all able-bodied men, and we have already fought decrepit, white-haired aged and buoyant, blithe boyhood."

And at another time, he waxes philosophic about his daily brush with death: "Man never knows his powers of endurance till he tries himself. The music of the enemy's balls is now as familiar and common as the carol of the spring bird which, unknowing of death and carnage around, sings today the same song that gladdened our forefathers."

But, of course, the thrust into the Midwest would ultimately end in the surrender of all of Morgan's command. While not all captured at once, McCreary was unfortunately one of the first, snared at Buffington Island, Ohio, as the Rebels were attempting to cross the Ohio River.

As McCreary described it, the ensuing battle was a ball of confusion: "The river was very full in consequence of a heavy rain away up the river. Shells and minnie balls were ricocheting and exploding in every direction, cavalry were charging, and infantry with its slow, measured tread moved upon us, while broadside after broadside was poured upon our doomed command from the gunboats. It seemed as if our comparatively small command would be swallowed up by the innumerable horde."

Transported first to Cincinnati, and then to Johnson Island, off the coast of Sandusky, Ohio, and finally incarcerated with Morgan at the Ohio State Penitentiary in Columbus, McCreary and his fellow prisoners at first lived a fairly comfortable life. They received visits from a sutler, from whom they bought certain necessities, but they also purchased other items to make them more comfortable in their surroundings, like beer, blankets, and "any necessary clothing." McCreary admitted that "friends have sent us large quantities of edibles and books, and we are doing as well as could be expected." In fact, he said that he had even "commenced the study of French, and with this and diverse, interesting books I manage to kill time pretty well."

But, of course, all that changed when Morgan and others escaped, leaving those unfortunate ones behind to be the object of the wrath of the prison officials and guards. McCreary, for example, said, "For 15 days all the officers have been locked in their cells, only coming out to meals. It is very trying and many are sick from the effects of the close encounters."

When they are finally allowed outdoors, McCreary observed that the confinement left the officers looking "ghostlike and ghastly." The food, too, was no longer acceptable; even Christmas dinner was in McCreary's words: "a ridiculous burlesque."

But McCreary's stay got even worse when the guards discovered a knife McCreary had hidden in the straw tick of his bed. For this infraction, he was thrown into the dark, dank dungeon where he was "confined for four days and nights, without fire and without covering," fed only "a half cup of water per diem and about one ounce of bread." He described the conditions as "this living death, this Hell on earth I endured for nearly five days, starving and walking day and night, and all the time nauseated by the terrible stench of a night bucket, which, though the only furniture in the cell, had seemingly not been cleaned for weeks."

When the days in the dungeon were done, he said, "I was scarcely able to stand up, and some of my comrades had to be helped to their cells, with their feet swollen and the blood oozing out under their fingernails and toe nails."

Finally, in late August, McCreary and 600 Confederate officers from Union prisons were chosen to be a part of one of the most diabolical military maneuvers of both the North and the South.

The facts are confusing, with both sides assigning blame to the other for the initiation of the action, and with each side claiming that it took the steps it did only to retaliate for what the other side had done.

At first, McCreary and the rest of the 600 thought they were bound for Charleston, South Carolina on the steamboat *Crescent City* to be exchanged, an unusual procedure for late in the war. By this time, Union General U.S. Grant had realized that the war could be won, in part, by attrition. In other words, he didn't like the idea of fighting the same Confederate soldiers again and again, who had been captured, paroled or exchanged, and then later showed up on the battlefield once more.

At any rate, Union commanders had for eighteen months relentlessly bombarded Charleston, the city so often associated with rebellion, the scene, in fact, of the very beginning volleys of the Civil War itself at Fort Sumter in the Charleston Harbor.

The shelling of Charleston was a merciless attack on this urban center of Southern charm, designed more to break the Southern spirit than to acquire land.

But here's where the stories each side tells conflict.

What is abundantly clear, however, is that the Union commanders believed that those defending Charleston were using Union prisoners of war as "human shields," strategically placing these hapless Boys in Blue in positions so that they, not the city's residents, would absorb the brunt of the Yankee bombardment.

To retaliate in this tit for tat arrangement, or so the other side says, the Union placed the recently transported McCreary and the other 600 Confederate officers on Morris Island, a small island in

Charleston Harbor from which the Union guns were shelling the city.

So, now, these Rebel officers had become a "human shield" also.

McCreary described the experience as a "ceaseless and continual bombardment...by two batteries in front of us and in rear of us, and to which our batteries [Confederate guns in Charleston] occasionally replied."

With shells dropping precariously over his head, McCreary somehow managed to compare the situation to a Fourth of July celebration: "We see Yankee shells passing over us and the shells of our friends passing in reverse direction, altogether making a grander and more imposing display of fireworks than I have ever beheld before."

But later, on September 10th, as the shelling continued, his thoughts about his plight turned bitter: "When and how this life will end is yet unwritten, but we all agree that such proceedings are unparalleled and barbarous."

In spite of all the shelling, when it was all over, not one of the 600 was killed, a fact that prompted one of the Confederate officers there, Major J. Ogden Murray, to title a book on their days on Morris Island *The Immortal Six Hundred*.

But even forty years after the war when Murray published his book, he was still bitter for the experience: "It was cowardly, it was inhuman, and cruel. The names of the men responsible for this cruelty must be written–and they will be written–upon history's blacklists of cruel men."

Adding to the malignancy of their stay on Morris Island were their daily rations, consisting of a scrawny ten ounces of bug-infested corn meal and "acid pickles." In fact, conditions worsened to the point that men were finally reduced to eating dogs and cats for protein, supplemented with the always-available mice and rats.

Murray's account, tinged with stinging and bitter sarcasm, is most telling: "...we reveled in dog meat. We had steaks, roasts, and soup. The meat was tender and white; but, reader, I do not commend dog meat as a daily food, but if you ever are so unfortunate as to be a prisoner of war in the hands of a Gen. J.G. Foster, living on retaliation rations, you will find in your hunger that dog meat is most excellent, indeed."

On November 29, 1863, McCreary's lengthy diary ends.

Records indicate that he was later exchanged and served out the rest of the war in the Virginia mountains under the command of Kentuckian General John Cabell Breckinridge.

By this time a lieutenant colonel, after the war McCreary returned to his home in Richmond, Kentucky, and began his long and storied career in politics. While in various offices, he worked hard for reconciliation between the North and South, while actively promoting veteran affairs for both ex-Union and Confederate soldiers.

Surprisingly, in spite of his horrendous Civil War experiences, the meager and unhealthy diet, and his spirit-sapping confinement, his obituary notes that he "retained his bodily and mental vigor until the last."

Yet very few today know about McCreary's Civil War experiences: where he served, where he fought, what he lived through. What is clear, though, is that because of his mind-boggling experiences, he could have lived the rest of his life with haunting memories and caustic anger.

But fortunately, for Kentucky and the nation, he did not.

James Bennett McCreary lies buried in a family plot, lot 54, in Richmond Cemetery beside Polly, his beloved parrot.

Confederate General Braxton Bragg and General John Cabell Breckinridge: Feuding, Fighting and Fidgeting during the Civil War

That Confederate General Braxton Bragg was an incompetent military commander is almost a cliché among Civil War scholars. Some claim that Bragg more than anyone else is responsible for the Confederate defeat in what was then called the West. But the criticism doesn't stop there.

Gerald McWhiney, a Bragg biographer, noted that Bragg "expressed his opinions on all occasions and all subjects in a most tactless manner. This was his way; he would always be outspoken, never able to conceal or moderate his views." As McWhiney records, a host of Civil War historians agree that Bragg had his problems. For example, Civil War historian Bruce Catton said Bragg as commander of the Army of Tennessee "was as baffling a mixture of high ability and sheer incompetence as the Confederacy could produce." T. Harry Williams said that "Bragg [did] not have the will to overcome the inertia of the war." Clifford Dowdey called Bragg "a psychotic warrior" who "at the ultimate test of committing an army to battle ...shrank from the decision." Lt. Colonel Joseph B. Mitchell in his interpretation of the Civil War, *Decisive Battles of the Civil War*, summarizes Bragg's problems: "The net result" was that "he was an intelligent, skillful planner but, in his execution of plans, he was his own worst enemy."

In truth, Bragg had a few defenders, and surely in some ways he has become what one of his supporters calls "a favorite whipping boy of historians." To his credit, Bragg often visited his men when they were in the hospital from illness or recovering from the wounds of war, but the rank and file often disliked him.

Ultimately, though, the most serious charge leveled against

Bragg was that he could not and did not elicit the devotion and respect of his officers, who often faulted Bragg and his military tactics in battle. The result was that Bragg was constantly feuding with his generals and spread such discontent that he rendered many of them ineffective.

Perhaps the most prominent officer Bragg failed to get along with was Kentuckian John Cabell Breckinridge, the former youngest vice president at the time under James Buchanan and later the Secretary of War in the Confederate cabinet.

General Braxton Bragg: A sour disposition, impatient and divisive, but a friend of C.S.A. President Jefferson Davis. Courtesy of the Kentucky Historical Society.

Breckinridge ran for president of the United States in 1860 on the Southern Democratic ticket and finished behind Lincoln, but polled more than his Southern rival John Bell, a candidate who sought to avoid the dissolution of the Union. Curiously, Breckinridge, in spite of his popularity and influence in Kentucky, failed to win the Commonwealth in that same election.

A descendant of the Breckinridge family of central Kentucky who carried a long and storied name in the political history of Kentucky, John Cabell Breckinridge is described by State Historian James Klotter as "well-proportioned and erect [;] the orator impressed audiences as a tall man, but face to face people found him not nearly as tall as they had expected. When speaking, he seemed to 'dilate to yet larger proportions.'"

Klotter continues: "The firm jaw, the raven-black hair and the unusual blue eyes enforced the feeling that here stood a special man." As a speaker, "every attribute of the orator was present, and the resonant, sympathetic voice carried to the full limits of the large audiences...."

Kentucky historian Lowell Harrison also speaks of Breckinridge's bearing: "His commanding presence and his powerful voice, and his beguiling personality attracted supporters...."

Breckinridge was surely a "special man," perhaps one of, if not the most important Kentuckian to join the Confederate cause in the fall of 1861, after months of indecision and reflection. He gave up his newly won seat in the U.S. Senate to become, upon the recommendation of another prominent Kentuckian, General Simon Bolivar Buckner, Brigadier General in the C.S.A. army. At the same time, Breckinridge was officially branded a "traitor" by his U.S. Senate colleagues. But Breckinridge firmly felt that the Republicans would unnecessarily usurp the rights of the individual states by freeing the slaves, whom Breckinridge saw as symbolizing the Southerner's state right to property.

For a time commanding the First Kentucky Brigade, better known as "Orphan Brigade," Breckinridge's first real action in the war was at the Battle of Shiloh, Tennessee on April 6, 1862, where, although the Confederates failed to achieve their goal against Union General U.S. Grant and his forces, Breckinridge, according to Harrison, was praised by Bragg: "Nobly won upon the field, with the hearty congratulations of Braxton Bragg."

It was an honor that would seem quite hollow to Breckinridge a few short years later.

Needless to say, Breckinridge and his men were itching to get back into Kentucky to sway its reluctant ones toward the Confederate cause. So when Bragg made plans to invade the Bluegrass State in the early fall of 1862, Breckinridge received the orders his men were waiting for. Out of Knoxville, Breckinridge and his men gleefully marched behind Bragg, headed for Old Kentucky.

Bragg and his army entered the Bluegrass State with wagon load after wagon load chuck full of guns to distribute to the men from Kentucky whom Kentucky General John Hunt Morgan had promised were just waiting to join up with the Rebels.

But Breckinridge's forces only made it to near the Kentucky border when they received the disappointing news that Bragg and his men were retreating out of Kentucky after the tactical Union victory at the Battle of Perryville on October 8, 1862, the wagon loads of guns largely undistributed and Bragg bitterly disappointed about the Kentuckians who failed to rally around the Southern cause. He wrote to President Jefferson Davis that in Kentucky for the Confederate cause, "The results were not what I expected. Enthusiasm runs high, but exhausts itself in words."

Some would argue that it was at this point that Bragg lost his faith in Kentucky in general and Kentucky Confederate generals in particular.

Bragg, of course, defended his retreat out of the Bluegrass State, arguing he withdrew from Kentucky because he wanted to feed his "starving Army." But others saw it differently, very differently, and blamed Bragg for losing the "Battle for Kentucky." Bragg could have won, they argued, but his tentativeness, and lack of aggression had once more squandered a golden opportunity.

The relationship between Bragg and Breckinridge began to deteriorate further when, much to Breckinridge's disfavor, Bragg ordered the execution of a Kentucky Confederate accused of desertion. The young soldier was actually on his way back to his unit after assisting his starving family back in the Bluegrass when captured. But that didn't matter to Bragg. He sought to make an example of the young man. Harrison notes that Bragg said: "Kentucky blood was much too feverish for the health of the army," and that he intended "to stop the corn-crackers' grumbling if he had to execute every man."

Some scholars have also argued that Bragg, a West Point graduate, held little regard for what he might have called "political generals," those who had secured rank because of their political connections, not for their strict military training, which, of course, they did not have. In Bragg's mind, Breckinridge may have fit that description.

But in Breckinridge's defense, many of his cohorts spoke highly of him. John B. Gordon, Harrison notes, saw Breckinridge as exhibiting "in a marked degree the characteristics of a great commander. He was fertile in resource, and enlisted and held the confidence and affection of his men, while he inspired them with enthusiasm and ardor. Under fire and extreme peril he was strikingly courageous, alert, and self poised." Conrad Wise Chapman, who served under Breckinridge in the "Orphan Brigade," indicates how Breckinridge was regarded by his men: "He was a splendid man in every respect and we all soon came to love him as a father."

According to many, then, Breckinridge may not have had the military training of Bragg, but he certainly was able to inspire when all that Bragg could do was fidget and fuss.

The relationship between Bragg and Breckinridge worsened at the Battle of Stones River (sometimes called the Battle of Murfreesboro) on December 31, 1862, and January 1, 1863. Bragg could have easily won the battle if he had attacked the angle of the Union line, but once again, when he had the enemy in his jaws, Bragg hesitated. In other words, Bragg fussed, fumed, and fidgeted, when he could have easily walked away a winner.

Yet Bragg ordered Breckinridge and his men to launch a spirited attack on the Federals. Breckinridge balked, arguing that his information was different from Bragg's. Forced to obey Bragg's orders, Breckinridge remarked in anger to another commander: "General Preston, this attack is made against my judgment and by the special orders of General Bragg. Of course, we all must try to do our duty and fight the best we can. But if it should result in disaster and I be among the slain, I want you to do justice to my memory and tell the people that I believed this attack to be very unwise and tried to prevent it."

General John C. Breckinridge: One of the few successful "political generals." Courtesy of the Kentucky Historical Society.

Ironically, Breckinridge and his men <u>did</u> drive the Federals back, just as Bragg had envisioned, but when the Federals retreated, the Confederates met a devastating and withering sweep of Federal fire from 58 guns under Major John Mendenhall and his men.

The result was a disaster: The Confederates lost one third of their men, and the retreat from Stones River began. Predictably, Bragg was critical of Breckinridge and his command after the battle. Some friends and fellow generals encouraged Breckinridge to resign in protest, or at least challenge the irascible Bragg to a duel, but Breckinridge did neither.

Bragg, sensing that many of his generals lacked faith in him as a commander, did something that reflects just how unaware he was of his status among these fellow warriors: He asked them to tell him if they had confidence in him as their commander.

It was an opening that many of his generals were looking for. General Patrick Cleburne and General William J. Hardee both expressed their lack of confidence in Bragg as their commander. Next, it was Breckinridge's turn: He began civilly, noting that his brigade commanders "request me to say that while they entertain the highest respect for your patriotism, it is their opinion that you do not possess the confidence of the army to an extent which will enable you to be useful as its commander. In this opinion I feel bound to state that I concur."

After some show of support from other members of the Confederate community, especially Bragg's friend, President Jefferson Davis, Bragg retained his position, albeit a tenuous one.

Several months later at Chattanooga, the relationship between Breckinridge and Bragg came completely unhinged when Bragg, as usual, was looking for somebody to blame for his army's poor showing. This time it was Breckinridge again. After the battle, Bragg filed a report that accused Breckinridge of the serious charge of drunkenness.

Bragg said that Breckinridge was intoxicated from November 23rd to November 27th, so drunk that he fell down on the floor. Bragg went on to contend that Breckinridge was also drunk at Stones River, a fact that significantly diminished the effectiveness of Bragg's entire army, so Bragg claimed. Few would deny that Breckinridge enjoyed his bourbon, he was a true Kentuckian and a Southern gentleman after all; but Breckinridge's biographer, William C. Davis, notes that "in all of Breckinridge's lifetime as a moderate drinker, Bragg was the only person ever to claim having seen him intoxicated." Davis argues that Breckinridge's wife Mary sent him brandy or porter on occasion, hardly something she would do if Breckinridge had a drinking problem. Davis also states that, according to all reports, Breckinridge was in full use of his faculties during the battle at Chattanooga and showed no signs of incapacitation.

True, Breckinridge died young at the age of fifty-four of cirrhosis of the liver, but as Davis notes, "while it cannot positively be denied that Breckinridge was drunk during those four days, Bragg's charge is hardly sufficient to warrant the assumption that the Kentuckian was under such influence. The commanding general's accusation is made all the more suspect" when Breckinridge's able leadership during this period of time is examined closely.

And, of course, what makes Bragg's charge even less credible is the general's belief in a year-long conspiracy to relieve him from command. Bragg had the proverbial axe to grind, a need for spiteful vengeance.

At any rate, in November of 1863, Bragg tendered his resignation to President Jefferson Davis and was replaced with General Joseph E. Johnston, and Bragg then assumed a position as military adviser to President Davis.

After several months of leave, Breckinridge was assigned to the Western Department of Virginia. After successfully defending the salt works at Saltville, Virginia, at New Market he won an impressive victory in May of 1864. He fought then at Cold Harbor and was a part of Jubal Early's unsuccessful raid on Washington, D.C.

On February 6, 1865, Davis appointed Breckinridge Secretary of War, an appointment almost meaningless near the end of the war when all seemed quite hopeless for the fledgling republic.

After the war, Breckinridge fled first to Cuba, toured much of Europe and the Holy Land, lived in Canada for a time, and returned for his last few years to his beloved Kentucky. He died quietly at home on May 17, 1875, as well respected and loved then as when he left Kentucky to fight for the Confederate cause.

Few laypersons know about Breckinridge's feud with Bragg. It is the measure of the man that Breckinridge didn't let the memories of the squabbles dominate his last few years and attempt to "right" the wrong he had been dealt. He was a fine commander who fought for a cause he believed in, in fact, fought nobly for that cause until defeated in arms, but not in spirit. One contemporary, Klotter, quotes a saying that when you were with him, "you were in the presence of true greatness and yet no one felt abashed, for his manner was so charming and natural that you liked him at once."

He was one of Kentucky's most distinguished politicians and generals, a fact Bragg in his myopia failed to recognize.

Confederate Captain Thomas Hines' Narrow Escape at Blue River Island in Lower Meade County

Many Kentuckians know that on July 7, 1863, Confederate General John Hunt Morgan and around 2,000 Rebels launched what historians called his The Great Raid by crossing the Ohio River into Yankeeland, at Brandenburg, a campaign that eventually became the deepest penetration into the North by the Confederacy during the Civil War.

Besides creating fear and havoc and destruction in areas that until that time felt safe from the war, a number of historians and Civil War buffs have speculated about just why Morgan dared to try such a risky raid.

One theory is that Morgan and his men invaded the North looking to link up in Pennsylvania with General Robert E. Lee after Lee's glorious victory at Gettysburg. Of course, Lee was not victorious in that small Pennsylvania town in a bloody battle with total casualties for both sides in excess of 50,000, but that could have been Morgan's intent.

What seems quite clear is that Morgan disobeyed his commander's orders by leaving the state of Kentucky. General Braxton Bragg was all too willing to approve Morgan's raid into Kentucky, but he told Morgan not to go any farther north.

Yet examining obscure and weathered documents in the Thomas Hines papers, located in the Margaret King Library at the University of Kentucky, may indeed provide some clues to answering the question of why Morgan so boldly ferried his men across the river at Brandenburg on the boats the *Alice Dean* and the *John T. McCombs* into Indiana. For it was a mission that led ultimately to most of the men and the general himself landing in the Ohio Penitentiary in Columbus.

Called by his Yankee counterparts, "The Most Dangerous Man in the Confederacy," Thomas H. Hines, a Butler County native and a college professor at Masonic College in LaGrange, left a camp near Albany, Kentucky on June 5, 1863, with about eighty men on what was described as a scouting mission into southern Indiana, on orders from Morgan. Some historians say Captain Hines was looking for fresh horses, an idea that makes some sense, as Morgan commanded a cavalry and needed healthy horses.

But there was another reason that Hines and his men on Saturday, June 17th, crossed the Ohio River between Rome and Derby, Indiana, roughly across from Stephensport, Kentucky in Breckinridge County.

That same reason helps to explain why Morgan began his bold mission so self-assured, but the possible explanation requires a bit of background.

First, much of southern Illinois, Indiana, and Ohio was settled by former Kentuckians. Abraham Lincoln, for example, was born in Kentucky, reared in Indiana, and then moved on to Illinois where most of his friends were originally from Kentucky. Of course, many other families, like the Lincolns, also moved into the southern parts of these Midwestern states.

Next, early settlers, although they now lived in the North, still harbored strong southern sympathies, even before the War between

A view of the Ohio River near where Blue River Island was until the Cannelton Dam.

the States. So when war broke out, a number of secret societies in one way or another aided the Confederate cause. Dubbed "Copperheads" by their enemies, these groups had a slew of different names: Knights of the Golden Circle, Order of the American Knights, and the Sons of Liberty, just to name a few.

But membership in these groups in the Midwest was substantial enough that the Lincoln Administration constantly worried about their presence and influence. Even county newspapers were suspected as being under the influence of these secret groups with special passwords, watchwords, and secret greetings—and their purpose, according to Governor Oliver Morton of Indiana, was "to give aid and comfort to the southern traitors."

Incidents involving violence flared up in various parts of the region and even affected the recruiting efforts of the U.S. Army desperate to fill their quotas.

With such a presence of these veiled organizations in the lower Midwest, it seems reasonable to conclude that Hines' foray into southern Indiana was designed, in part at least, to see just how much support Morgan and his men would have for their jaunt into the North.

Historian Orlando Willcox in his account of part of The Great Raid says that Morgan believed that "his ranks would be at least largely recruited in the southern counties of Indiana," where these secret organizations were "the strongest." Second in command to Morgan, General Basil Duke, said later in life that Morgan and his men "expected" that they would garner support from those of southern sympathies in the parts of the Midwest they invaded.

On June 7th, then, on the Kentucky side of the Ohio River opposite near Rome, Indiana, Hines and his men, estimated by some reports to be as many as 500 and by others at only 62, found an old boat that his men bailed out, and after several trips, the troop was in Indiana, heading for the junction of the Ohio and Mississippi Railroad, where there was a military commissary store with supplies any military man would want.

Hines then explained to his men that they would pose as "Indiana Greys," a company with similar colors to Hines' own, supposedly looking for deserted and absentee Union soldiers. Hines would be known as Captain Scott. But they didn't get far, for soon they were attacked by the Home Guards (local military units). Hines and his men, however, soon drove the locals off in various directions.

Gradually, Hines and his force made it near Paoli, where he learned that the news of his real identity was now out, and that a large force ahead of him, behind him, and at his left and right flanks had all gathered, intent upon capturing the invading Rebels.

In a clever sleight of hand, Hines somehow captured one of the enemy and used him as a guide. In the dark night, amid confusion created by Hines' derring-do, he and his men managed to elude their would-be captors, and Hines and company headed south for the river, employing still another local resident along the way to help Hines find an escape route.

Traveling all night, they reached the Ohio at about 10:00 the next morning, near Leavenworth, Indiana, a small river town then that has since moved to higher ground after the 1937 flood. Opposite Leavenworth were two islands, the larger of the two referred to as Blue River Island, large enough in the twentieth century for farming, but barely visible now after the opening of the Cannelton Locks and Dam in 1967 that swallowed up the second, smaller island.

On the Kentucky side of the river, the two islands were some distance before the river makes its radical two bends in this part of lower Meade County.

With two companies of Home Guards close behind, Hines and his men made for Blue River Island and set up an ambush for those approaching and for capturing the first steamboat to happen by to ferry them to the Kentucky side.

Soon a steam tug chugged by, and after a few shots through the pilot house, Hines' men prepared to capture the boat.

But at that moment, the Home Guards, several hundred strong, suddenly came into sight, along with a Yankee gun boat that began peppering the island with gunshots.

Waiting until the Yankees were in plain sight, Hines and his men "poured a volley into" the Yankee position, driving them back.

The Yankees tried it again, and again were driven back.

With the gun boat now continuing to fire into the island and with Home Guard reinforcements arriving, and with the Rebels quickly running out of ammunition, Hines turned to the captured tug boat as a way out of the perilous predicament, only to see that in the confusing action, it had taken off.

That left only two options: Hines and his men could surrender, or they could break for the Kentucky shore. Fearing capture, they mounted their horses in a desperate attempt to escape, and plunged into the river. But the horses soon floundered, drowning several men and their mounts.

Returning to the island briefly, Hines told his men that he was "going to swim the river and called upon all who preferred freedom to confinement in a Yankee prison to follow him."

Some twelve to fifteen men followed his lead, all stripped of their clothes, with bullets flying all around and "bursting shells" exploding above them.

Hines managed to retain two pistols by holding them above the water, and took along his watch and money by placing them in his hat. When he reached the Kentucky shore, he waved his hat in proud defiance at the Yankees on the other shore, while his men on the island cheered, but shortly those remaining on the island were Yankee prisoners.

Hines procured some clothing for himself and his men from someone living near the river, but all barefooted, and most hatless, they walked some eight miles along the rocky ridges from Big Bend to "a house on a hill," possibly close to Stapleton, near present-day Battletown, where Hines suspected a Rebel sympathizer lived.

Revealing his true identity, he asked for assistance, but the woman of the house turned out to be a strong Union supporter; yet somehow Hines, gifted with natural charm, persuaded the woman not to report him and his men.

She even provided him with a guide to take the group to a southern sympathizer inland about seven miles, where he and his men secured clothes, horses, arms, and boots for his "sore-footed men."

Hines says that he and his men stayed in the area until June 27th, when they struck out for Elizabethtown, Bardstown, Shelbyville, and Taylorsville, eventually robbing a train near Christianburg for needed money, and linking back up with Morgan in Brandenburg.

In fact, Hines and his remaining men were waiting for Morgan and his troops when they entered town at about nine the morning of July 7, 1863.

But his attempt to find southern supporters in Southern Indiana had failed. General Basil Duke admitted later that Morgan and his men did not receive any assistance from the many secret society members along the way in Indiana and Ohio.

Hines was among those captured along with Morgan on July 26th, outside of West Point, Ohio, near the Pennsylvania state line, effectively ending Morgan's Great Raid.

But Hines wasn't finished. He also was the mastermind behind Morgan's daring escape from the Ohio prison. Later, Hines came up with a bold plan to free Confederate prisoners from Chicago and Rock Island and lead the Midwest into union with the Confederacy, referred to by historians as the Great Northwest Conspiracy.

Of course, the plan failed, but by that time Thomas Hines had well earned his reputation as one of most resourceful and boldest men in the Confederacy, who, one late June day, narrowly escaped capture on Blue River Island in lower Meade County.

Kentuckian Thomas Henry Hines and the Northwest Conspiracy

Few figures in Civil War history rival Kentuckian and Confederate Captain Thomas Henry Hines for sheer daring, ingenious planning and irresistible charm.

He remains, though, generally unrecognized and under appreciated as a potent force in the Confederate military arsenal.

According to the *Kentucky Encyclopedia*, Hines was born on October 9, 1838, in Butler County, Kentucky. From 1859 to 1861, he taught at Masonic University in La Grange, Kentucky.

Other sources, particularly Stephen Z. Starr, say that Hines at the outbreak of the Civil War, was a classical scholar who quickly resigned his position and organized a troop of 15 men in Lexington, serving for a time under General Albert Sidney Johnston, who assigned him and his men to scouting, bridge-burning and other important duties. After a period of time when Hines was not in the Rebel Army, Hines re-enlisted and began his service under fellow Kentuckian General John Hunt Morgan in May of 1862.

Hines soon earned a solid reputation for undercover, behind-the lines assignments where he made contact, according to Starr, with Southern sympathizers, especially in the Old Northwest, contacts that served him well throughout the war.

Descriptions of Hines characterize him, among other things, as a John Wilkes Booth look-alike.

Duane Schultz's book on the Dahlgren Affair portrays Hines as five feet nine inches tall, about 140 pounds in weight, and with "long black curly hair, a bushy mustache, and dark slanting eyebrows."

One acquaintance described him as "modest, courteous, and

imperturbable, with a voice as soft as that of a refined woman."

But as Schultz makes clear, Hines' most outstanding characteristic was not his good looks, but his highly contagious and considerable charm, which he made great use of on several occasions.

Choosing to risk capture so that his commander, General John Hunt Morgan, could escape, Hines managed to talk himself out of two hangings by two different Yankee patrols.

But he was also decidedly a man of action. He could and did devise elaborate, and many times workable, schemes, just when the moment called for it.

For example, generally, Hines has been given credit for both concocting and carrying out the brilliant escape of Morgan and many of his men from the Columbus, Ohio prison they had been shamefully assigned to.

According to the legend—and there are certainly doubters—Hines and his men dug a tunnel with a broken pocket knife and some stolen kitchen utensils, a project that took a mere twenty days.

Hines could not resist the temptation, however, to goad the prison warden with a stinging message pinned to a straw-stuffed dummy. Schultz quotes Hines this way:

> Castle Merion, Cell No. 20
> Commencement, November 4, 1863
> Conclusion November 24, 1863
> Number of hours for labor per day: five;
> Tools, two small knives
> La patience est amere, mas son
> Fruit est doux. [Patience is sour,
> but its fruit is sweet.]
> By order of my six honorable
> Confederates,
>
> T.H. Hines
> Captain, C.S.A.

Yet in spite of all his derring-do, including such guerrilla activity as burning bridges and creating general havoc in parts of Kentucky, Hines' shining moment was supposed to be later in the war, when he was to execute a plan prompted by an event that struck terror and disgust in the heart of the Confederacy: the Dahlgren Affair.

Briefly summarized, the Dahlgren Affair revolves around a Union

Thomas H. Hines: College professor and General John Hunt Morgan's sly scout. Courtesy of the Kentucky Historical Society.

plot, to be carried out by Captain Ulric Dahlgren, a young man well known by President Abraham Lincoln, to free prisoners housed in deplorable conditions in Libby Prison in Richmond, Virginia, capital of the Confederate States of America. The mission began on the morning of February 28, 1864.

Ulric's father was Admiral John Dahlgren, an important military figure in Lincoln's Navy.

The mission failed, but more importantly, Rebel soldiers found a set of detailed instructions on the dead body of Captain Dahlgren that outlined, supposedly, plans to assassinate President Jefferson Davis and important members of his cabinet.

In a time when war was thought to be many times a gentleman's affair, the orders sent collective shivers down the backs of the entire Confederacy. War wasn't supposed to be like this. There were, after all, clear-cut rules of engagement. Assassinating a country's leaders was not supposed to happen.

According to Schultz, the *Richmond Enquirer* howled: "Soldiers, read these papers and weigh well their purpose and design....Should our army again go into the enemy's country, will not these papers relieve them from their restraints of chivalry that would be proper with a civilized enemy...." Calling the enemy, "a savage foe," the editorial concludes that the Dahlgren papers "will destroy during the rest of the war, all rosewater chivalry...."

From that point on in the war, the editorial advised that the Confederates would "make war afar and upon the rules selected by the enemy."

So wounded and outraged was the Confederacy that when Captain Hines met with Jefferson Davis during the second week in March of 1864 with a plan "to win the war," Davis was an eager listener, especially since the war was going badly, the South was in shambles, and runaway inflation seemed to be starving the fledgling republic. Hines' plan seemed the perfect reprisal for the Dahlgren Affair.

Although Davis found Hines' plan quite alluring, Davis had heard the premise of the plan before, but then the president was not as desperate as he was now. Davis needed some way to breathe life into a faltering Confederacy, and Hines' reputation for successful operations certainly preceded him.

In short, the plan, known as "The Northwest Conspiracy," was simple. Hines would go to Canada where many escaped Rebel veterans now lived, organize them into a fighting unit, and use them, and other Southern sympathizers, called Copperheads, to free the Southern soldiers held in Union prisons in Chicago and Rock Island, Illinois. These troops then would be accompanied by the other Copperheads in Illinois, Ohio, and Indiana, who would join the ex-prisoners in wreaking havoc in the Old Northwest. Such actions would then lead to the succession of these states from the Union. Subsequently, these same states and other states from the Northwest would join the Confederacy to form a new nation.

The term "Copperhead," is a slippery one. As it is usually used, a Copperhead was a person in the North, usually a resident of what is now called the Midwest, who sympathized with the states that joined the Confederacy, and was, ostensibly, willing to put forth any effort to aid the Southern cause. The most ardent believers organized themselves into secret societies such as Knights of the Golden Circle, Order of American Knights, and later, the largest in membership, The Sons of Liberty, so-called "black lantern" societies. In an article in *The Filson Club History Quarterly*, Starr notes that at the time of the war 40% of the residents of the Old Northwest were of Southern birth or parentage, which translates to substantial Southern sympathy. The Old Northwest was largely agricultural, too, meaning that residents depended heavily on agriculture, much as the South did. This agricultural emphasis was often at great odds with the Northeast, which depended more on manufacturing and trade and saw the South in an entirely different way.

As Hines read it, then, the Old Northwest would, if given the right opportunity, readily side with the South, for citizens of the Old Northwest were fed up with their treatment by the Lincoln administration, a truly questionable assumption that Hines built his hopes on.

Assisted by another Rebel, John Castleman, Hines, after careful deliberation with Davis and members of his cabinet, made his way to Canada by the middle of April of 1864. Schultz notes that at a banquet honoring Hines the night before he left, Hines made a bet that on his way through Washington, D.C. he could shake the hand of President Lincoln while Hines had the bonds to finance the mission sticking out of his pocket.

As Starr tells it, John Thompson of Mississippi also traveled to Canada with $900,000 to underwrite the cost of the project. The money was to cover the cost of arming those Confederate soldiers and provide transportation and living expenses to all involved in the operation.

The huge amount of money for that day says much about the faith the Confederate government had in the project. But it also says how desperate the same government was for some way to turn the war around, for the Confederacy was steadily sliding toward destruction.

The details that Hines, Davis and his cabinet, and Thompson worked out were to focus the attack on the Union prisons in Chicago on July 4, 1864, the date of the Democratic Convention, a time when lots of strangers in the Windy City would draw no undue attention. Besides, many Democrats in the Old Northwest had expressed views about the war quite different than those of the Lincoln administration.

But when Hines began the mechanics of organizing the raid, he found that the organization of the Copperheads, especially of the Sons of Liberty, was in disarray, so the raid was re-scheduled, after several times, for August 29th.

The master plan was to free the prisoners in Camp Douglas in Chicago, free the prisoners in Rock Island, move on and free the prisoners in Columbus, Ohio and Indianapolis, and take over the respective governments in Illinois, Indiana, and Ohio.

Unfortunately, the Union had spies in several places and by the time the date of execution of the plan was to take place, the Union forces had learned of the plan. By November 8th, the last date the parties agreed upon, the government had arrested key leaders and thwarted what little enthusiasm and planning the principals had left.

Starr says that the Northwest Conspiracy failed mainly because "for all their loud talk, the Copperhead leaders were found wanting when the day for action came; they simply lacked the courage of their convictions."

Writing some twenty-four years after the aborted mission, Hines himself was perhaps more gracious in his explanation of why the mission failed: "It soon developed that the men employed for gathering the members of the order had not faithfully performed their duties, and that the preparation for immediate and open hostilities to the administration had destroyed the confidence or dissipated the courage of some of the men whose leadership was necessary."

The Northwest Conspiracy had not come to fruition. In point of fact, the plan had been a miserable failure.

The Confederate government had invested money and time and hope, but all for naught.

Historian James Ramage records that Hines began a practice of law in Bowling Green, two years after the war. Elected to the Court of appeals in 1878, he stepped up to Chief Justice in 1884 and served until 1886. He passed away on January 23, 1898.

Except for the failure of the Northwest Conspiracy and his and Morgan's escape from the Columbus prison, not much is said about this clever man with the charming disposition.

But few who know of him fail to recognize his rightful place in Civil War history.

THE FEEDING OF THE HORDES: THE CIVIL WAR AND THE SHAKERS AT PLEASANT HILL

The great French nineteenth century military leader, Napoleon Bonaparte, is quoted as saying, "an army marches on its stomach."

That observation was certainly true in Europe at the time, and it fit with the circumstances of the American Civil War, too.

With more than three million men and several hundred women bearing arms during the four-year conflict, one soldier's comment about the need for food seems particularly apt: "It's hard to maintain one's patriotism on ashcake and water."

While the Union army was generally well fed, the Confederates fought a war-long battle with hunger both at home and in the field.

According to Michael J. Varhola in his book, *Everyday Life during the Civil War*, shortages were worse in the cities where food was generally not produced and prices became ridiculously inflated. By 1865, in Richmond, for example, bacon sold for as much as $13 a pound, a pound of butter went for up to $20 a pound, and corn meal topped out at $400 a bushel. People in the rural areas, who were used to growing and gathering food, often fared much better, in spite of a wide-spread and essentially eroded infrastructure.

Food for the average Civil War soldier was not a very appetizing fare. For the Union soldier, the main course was hardtack, a salted cracker made of flour and water. The main advantage of hardtack was its durability. It resisted many insects from feeding on it, and mice and rats didn't like it either. To dress up hardtack, many Boys in Blue dunked it in their coffee or soaked it in water, added bacon or pork grease, and fried it. "Hellfire stew," "lobcourse," or "skillygalee" were just some of the lighthearted names soldiers gave to their concoctions. Confederate soldiers were given an allotment of cornmeal that they used to make a cornbread to which they added salt pork or bacon drippings. Both sides added fruit and vegetables when they could get them along their way. In essence, the diet of both Union and Confederate soldiers was not something the soldiers approached with much gusto.

As a result, the average Confederate soldiers and some Union soldiers were often underfed and malnourished, evidencing diseases like rickets, diarrhea, and other maladies, which resulted from poor or insufficient diets.

Such deficiencies led to widespread foraging for food in the field, a practice called "pressing," which *The Encyclopedia of Civil War Usage* defines as "slang, for impressment, which involved the seizure of horses, vehicle, supplies and other material needed by armies in the field. Previous owners were often given receipts, but few were ever honored." Other terms were also used, many humorously, considering the dire circumstances. According to Varhola, one such was "slow bear" which referred to a "lighthearted term used by foraging troops to refer to the farmers' pigs that they killed and ate." "Mud lark" was another humorous term, which referred to "domestic pigs they killed and ate. Presumably, the farmers who owned these pigs," Varhola concludes, "were not as amused as the soldiers."

Other soldiers also saw a lighter side to "pressing." J.S. Robb, a Rebel writing to his brother, added that, "These Arkansas hoosiers ask from 25 to 30 cents a pound for [their] pork, but the boys generally get it a *little cheaper* than *that*. I reckon you understand how they get it."

Even at the highest levels of command, there was good-natured kidding about "pressing." General Robert E. Lee said of Confederate General John Bell Hood, "Ah, General Hood, when you Texans come about the chickens have to roost mighty high."

Yet with all lightheartedness aside, however, feeding so many starved soldiers was a real problem most of the time for the Confederates, and some of the time for even the Union soldiers.

So when a place like Pleasant Hill appears on the dusty horizon for hundreds of hungry soldiers, North and South, it looked too good to be true.

Pleasant Hill, or Shakertown, was alluring for a number of reasons.

In an article on the Pleasant Hill Shakers and the Civil War in *The Harrodsburg Herald* in 1998, Susan Lyons Hughes correctly observes that "the location of the village along the busy Lexington, Nashville, and Zanesville Turnpike and near the Kentucky River, however, made the community of Shakers particularly vulnerable when civil war broke out in 1861."

In other words, being too "handy" for a steady stream of hungry soldiers to feed, especially when the farm offered over 2,800 acres and fed 600 people anyway. The temptation just was too great.

At the same time, there is another, more compelling reason that soldiers stopped at Pleasant Hill, and that was that the soldiers knew they would not be turned away. They may not get all they wanted, but they would be fed.

That was because the Shakers held some very strong sentiments about charity and service to humankind.

Basically, the Shakers, an offshoot of the Quakers, called "Shaking Quakers" for the dances and movements they performed during worship services in a kind of religious ecstasy, believed in the possibility of human perfectibility here on earth, and Pleasant Hill was such an experiment.

In Julia Neal's book on the Shakers here in Kentucky, she outlines their basic tenets. One of several beliefs was that Shakers did not

A view of Shakertown: Keeping both sides fed was a constant worry for the pacifist Shakers at Pleasant Hill. Courtesy of the Kentucky Historical Society.

hold earthly possessions. All things were kept in common by the community, but at the same time the Shakers worked very hard to be "honest in the sight of men" and lay up in store provisions for the honor of God and the relief and succor of him that needeth."

Consequently, not to feed the hungry would be a violation of their religious code. In other words, they were bound by their belief to feed the hungry no matter who they were.

Neal notes, for example, that as the war widened the Shakers "were actually to be victimized by their own reputation of being a generous and charitable people who, in accordance with their millennial law, never turned anyone away who needed help."

One Shaker described serving the soldiers: "All our hand labor is pretty much suspended, and the greater number of us are engaged in service for the army. The Brethren are actively engaged in hauling wood and attending to the various calls for the soldiers. The Sisters are cooking, baking, etc., trying to keep the house in some degree of order and decency."

Another noted, "It is now near nine o'clock p.m. The Brethren are away attending to the soldiers and we are all alone."

But the plight of the soldiers must have milked mercy from the Shakers. One observer noted that they "devoured the raw lettuce with avidity; they surrounded our wells like the locusts of Egypt... and they struggled with each other for water as if perishing with thirst... they thronged our kitchen doors... begging for bread like hungry wolves. We nearly emptied our pantries of their contents and they tore the loaves and pies into fragments, devouring them."

Surely, too, the Shakers also recognized that feeding the hundreds was also an act of survival for the Shakers themselves. Neal observes that supplying food "would save more by being kind and accommodating than they would lose."

Neal notes that this attitude did hold up because as one Shaker said, "the soldiers behaved quietly and orderly and made no depredations, or they might play two handsome tunes, swing their hats, and cheer for the Shakers."

Neal also says that even when soldiers offered to pay, the Shakers turned it down, setting "limits, serving only such as" they could "afford." But they had to be careful when they rang the dinner bell, "for fear of a rush from the multitudes of the famishing."

One of the greatest fears that the Shakers faced was the fear of

Confederate raider John Hunt Morgan and his men. As Thomas Clark describes in his book on the Shakers at Pleasant Hill, "rumors preceded Morgan," predicting "all sorts of dire circumstances. Morgan's men would burn the village, steal the horses, and rob the stores." So in anticipation, the Shakers hid the horses and other provision they thought Morgan and his men would confiscate, something described by one Pleasant Hill resident as a "stampede of mules and horses to escape Rebel clutches."

Julia Neal quotes one Shaker who was told that "General Morgan informed us that he and his command had intended taking up lodging with us but that our generosity had induced him to move further on to avoid oppressing us. Two of the company attempted to press a horse a piece but a counter order from the General prevented [it]."

Another group, this time Union soldiers, also showed their civil side. Hughes quotes from a Shaker diary entry for August 17, 1862: A company of 100 United States Cavalry, in transit, encamped in our pasture, east of the East Barn. We gave them supper and breakfast in the office yard, and fed their horses at the camp, and gave them lunch when they left at noon today, they having been ordered back to Harrodsburg. They behaved civilly, being quiet and orderly, and committing no depredations, and made polite demonstrations of gratitude on taking leave..."

One of the particularly taxing days was October 11, 1862, after the Battle of Perryville, some seventeen miles away, sometimes called "The Battle for Kentucky." According to Hughes, on October 11, 10,000 Confederate soldier make their way through Pleasant Hill. In all, the Shakers fed about 1,000 soldiers. One Shaker noted that "such a day as this has never been witnessed on Pleasant Hill before, and God grant that it never may again.... A temporary table in the office yard was kept almost constantly filled during the day so that we have fed more than a thousand persons today. And yet they beg food and clothing, and almost every thing used for the comforts of life." With soldiers, "as far as the eye could see," the Shakers "served out their rations, which occupied two hours or more. During this time, the Sisters were cooking and baking with all means at their command..." The Shaker observes in disgust: "How awful to think of a wicked and bloody battle occurring in the midst of Zion on earth!"

All told, as Clark says, "from July 1, 1862, until the end of the war, Pleasant Hill was not again to experience freedom from anxiety and fright caused by troop movements and guerrilla raids." On September 6th, 7th, and 8th Rebels appeared in the thousands begging for food. Life in the peaceful village was chaotic with all these new troops to feed.

One elder Clark quotes intoned, "O God! Protect this heritage from the ravages of cruel war." Things got so bad that residents put up a temporary table and graced it with food everyday. Clark notes that "the theme of daily entries in the village journal had come to have a monotony, soldiers, work, begging, exhaustion, and the roar of war.

There is little doubt that by war's end all this feeding would take its toll.

These gentle and generous people were indeed supremely affected by their largess. After the Civil War, the Shakers, who had shipped their products South, found that those markets, because of the war, were no longer financially solvent enough to buy the seeds, preserves, hams, medicines, and seeds the Shakers produced. The years after the war also saw the mechanization of industry in other parts of the country so that the Shakers could no longer manufacture brooms and other products at prices to compete with those mass-produced by burgeoning industries. Noting all these factors, Clark concludes, "the Civil War had an enormous impact on Pleasant Hill."

Flo Morse's study echoes Clark, concluding that the "Civil War placed a heavy burden on the Shaker communes in Kentucky, drained their strength, destroyed their markets, and distracted them from their religious goals. They were the victims of their own charity, unable to deny food, supplies and lodging to the insistent, and ruthless soldiers of both the Union and Confederate armies."

The limitless larder that Pleasant Hill had become during the war may not have been the sole determiner of the gradual but steady decline of this utopian community, but supplying so much food to so many hastened the gradual decline of an experiment in human community that had proved in previous years to be so promising.

THE WAR ON THE HOME FRONT: LEXINGTON, KENTUCKY

Civil War historians often cite Kentucky as one state where brother did truly fight brother during the war. As Lowell Harrison and James Klotter in their history of Kentucky observe, one example of brother against brother is the prominent Crittenden family of Western Kentucky, where brother Thomas fought for the Union, while brother George fought for the Gray. In the Breckinridge family of Central Kentucky, two of Robert Breckinridge's sons fought for the Union, and two fought on the side of the Rebels. Individual families were torn apart, too. George Prentice, editor of the generally Union Louisville newspaper, *The Journal*, had two sons who sided with the Confederacy. Samuel McDowell Starling from Hopkinsville sided with the Union army, and had one son killed fighting for the North, and one killed in action supporting the South.

Kentucky was also a state where part of a town supported the Union, while other parts were Southern in their sympathies. For example, Brandenburg in Meade County as well as other small towns all across Kentucky had one part of the city leaning toward the North while another favored the Confederacy.

Imagine the awkwardness, anger and sheer frustration of knowing that your next-door neighbor wanted nothing more than your side's defeat, even sending sons to possibly give their lives to defeat your sons in battle.

But what about these noncombatants, the children and wives and women at home? How did they feel about the war? How did they fare? Or how were they affected by the internecine conflict?

Not much is out there to delineate the effects of the war on those at home, a topic receiving more and more attention these days by historians. So we are fortunate in Kentucky to have the extensive record of a young, perceptive woman in Lexington who, for most of the war, chronicled not only what she saw, but also how she felt about life during the war around the Bluegrass.

Published in 2000 by the University Press of Kentucky, *A Union Woman in Civil War Kentucky*, edited by John David Smith and William Cooper, Jr., is the revealing and often poignant record of nineteen year-old Frances Peter. With a keen eye and telling details, the epileptic daughter of a Union surgeon and prominent Lexington physician recorded what was happening all around her. The diary begins January 19, 1862 and ends on April 4, 1864, important and active years for the war in Kentucky.

What stands out most obviously about the diary is the truly divided nature of Lexington during the War, the almost daily struggles of neighbor against neighbor in Central Kentucky.

In her diary, Ms. Peter splits those with Southern sympathies into three categories: Copperheads, secesh, and rebels.

"Copperhead" is a pejorative term for Northern Democrats who leaned toward compromise with the South, a stance toward the war that Peter saw as totally unacceptable. One time she brands Richard Buckner's speech as "being rather Copperhead." Another time she assails the Lexington newspaper *The Observer and Reporter* for favoring "Copperhead ideas." She is indeed a staunch Unionist, but she is a staunch Unionist with a Kentucky brand.

She terms neighbors who openly display their Southern leanings as "secesh," a shortened form of "secessionist." Among other things, she talks about the "secesh" ladies that gather together for mutual support.

Not surprisingly she saves special condemnation for the "secesh" Henrietta Morgan, mother of Confederate General John Hunt Morgan and five other brothers fighting for the South. At one time, Mrs. Morgan's house becomes the object of a search by a Union officer who is convinced that some of Morgan's men are hiding. However, Mrs. Morgan insists, on her honor, that there is no one inside, but a servant alerts the officer, to Frances Peter's delight, that the man in question was trying to escape. Peter then advises the reader to Mrs. Morgan as the mother of the "notorious John H. Morgan."

Another time, Peter notes that, "fuel is very scarce, at least for

Union people. Coal sells for 75 cents a bushel and hardly to be got for love or money. The secesh are keeping it all for themselves. They say that last week 400 bushels have been delivered daily at Mrs. Morgan's," she says with acid in her voice.

She also observes one time that "some one was arrested at Mrs. Morgan's this evening," from which Ms. Peter garners great satisfaction.

"We heard a good story of Mrs. Morgan today," she begins. "She went to headquarters saying she had heard several of southern mails had been intercepted...." One of the letters contained directions for sending "some clothes she had promised to send...and where to send them. Mrs. Morgan, of course, was very angry. A good many mails and mail carriers have lately been intercepted passing between the rebels here and their friends in Dixie."

Peter's attitude toward Rebels, that is, the soldiers doing the fighting, is quite caustic and intransigent, too. One time when Rebel soldiers dressed in Union uniforms to try to hide their identity, she remarks that "it looks so strange to see some of the dirty rebels and they seem to be ashamed of it too, for if any one remarks upon it, they hang their heads and hurry by pretending not to hear." Another time, she comments on the "cowardice" of the rebels. Still later, she says that "they keep themselves and everything so dirty." And at another time, she brands the Rebels "a pack of curs." She also accuses the Rebels of burning the houses in Mount Sterling and bayoneting "eight or ten sick who were there and then burnt the buildings with the bodies in them."

Finally, she quips that "the Richmond papers are urging the propriety of killing all the dogs in the Confederacy as they consume too much bread. It would be a good thing if they would kill all the two-legged as well as the four-legged ones."

Not surprisingly for the average slaveholder in Kentucky, at the same time, Peter also holds some hatred for Abolitionists. At one point she remarks that "the draft has put so many Abolitionists and mean men in the Regiments that the Generals have almost if not more trouble with them than with the secesh."

In the end, she is able to make a fine distinction between being a slave owner, yet still supporting the Union cause.

Her attitudes toward African Americans is paternal or custodial at best, commenting one time that an African American, "is much too averse to work, too timid to make a good soldier, and has gotten into his head that liberty means doing nothing." Later, she says that, "in fact, the negroes throughout the country are no longer the humble servants that they used to be. They are restless, impertinent and disconnected, neglect their work, and run off in great numbers."

At the same time, Peter also harbors great fear of Blacks, arguing that after Lincoln authorized the recruitment of Black soldiers: "I am afraid now the negroes have got arms in their hands, and so many notions of freedom in their heads that before the war is over it is not improbable that we may have to fight them as well as the secesh."

But a mere four months later, she seems reconciled to the idea that the African Americans will be freed: "It is an undoubted fact that we are much nearer emancipation now, than even last year. People are getting accustomed to the idea, and do not think it near as terrible as they used to." Later, she echoes these remarks, saying, "I for one would not be at all disgusted at having [Kentucky] slaves emancipated."

Yet she seems a bit surprised in November of 1863, when she reads in a local newspaper about Abolitionist Henry Ward Beecher's speech in which he argued that the war's purpose then was to abolish slavery and that the war, "be continued (even after the rebels have surrendered) until slavery is utterly exterminated from the country. Now, I always understood that this war was undertaken merely to put down rebellion." She continues, "But to say that this war is carried on for the purpose of abolishing slavery is to give the rebels just cause of complaint and give them a strong point to base their case on. The rebels say, 'the Yankee government is fighting to take away our negroes.'"

Peter then concludes that, "Now I think with [Kentucky] Governor Bramlette that a man who won't have the Union, unless the negroes are out of it, is just as bad and as much an enemy to the Union cause, as the secessionist who won't have the Union unless he can have the negro too.

For my part, I say whip the rebels first and then let the ballot box decide the slavery question if there are any slaves left."

Thus, she seems resigned to Lincoln's being re-elected, noting that, "We did not think much of him at first and he only got one vote in Lexington, but the more we see of him the better we like him."

Yet one of the most interesting observations to be gleaned from the Peter diary is the constant parade of troops both North and South that occupy the Bluegrass. Besides Southern troops like Confederate General John Hunt Morgan whose men make numerous forays in the area, and Confederate General Kirby Smith and his men, Union troops come from all parts of the country. Besides the Boys in Blue from Kentucky, Peter also lists troops from East Tennessee, Missouri, Ohio, Illinois, Maryland, Rhode Island, Michigan, Wisconsin, Indiana, Illinois, and Pennsylvania, among others.

With so much attention, it is clear how important Kentucky was to the Union cause. At one point, Peter says, "More troops came in today. I cannot find out how many troops are here now, they are continually going and coming, and it is hard to find out when they go, where to or anything about them."

One revealing sidelight of the Peter diary is a report she quotes from a Paducah newspaper. According to the correspondent, letters from the wives of captured Confederate soldiers expressed frustration and anger at their men for having been away from home so long. One woman, for example, writes to her husband: "You have wanted to be in this war since it began, and I reckon you will get your fill before it is done. I have my fill already. I am willing to have peace in any way." She continues, "Oh! I would give anything I possess, or ever expect to, if you hadn't gone in this war. If I had known everything as I do now I would have tied you and kept you tied to have made you know I never did want you to go."

Then, she lists her troubles, "I tell you it makes me feel awful to think that I will be left in the world with two little children with no way to make a support." Finally, she concludes, "I can't see what all the women will do if all the men are taken from here. I am more troubled now than I ever have been."

Such a letter lends credence to the idea that support in the South from home began to wane as the war wore on, something no doubt true in the North also.

It is difficult to overestimate the value of the Peter diary in understanding what the war was like on the home front, especially in the Bluegrass. Without her careful and extensive notes, we would miss much that would help us understand just how disruptive and agonizing the war was in the Bluegrass. For the words of a young woman in Civil War Lexington bring to life just how terrible the irrepressible conflict was, and how it so adversely affected even the people back home.

Life for Kentuckians at Camp Douglas, a Civil War Prison

Historians and lay persons alike have written much about the awful conditions at Camp Sumter, better known as Andersonville for its location in Andersonville, Georgia, the South's most notorious prisoner of war camp. After the Civil War, the death and the disease were also much a part of the legend that ultimately led to the hanging of the prison's commander, Major Henry Wirz, C.S.A., for war crimes.

Writing of Andersonville, George Levy describes the conditions there as "a garbage pit, a giant maggot that swallowed men without malice.... Andersonville was barren of expectations because it was without hope." Without enough to feed even its own soldiers, the South supplied the camp with little food, medicine and other resources, and men died in droves from starvation and rampant disease.

Adding to the high mortality rate at Andersonville was the fact that prisoners well enough to travel were often sent to other prisons, while the sickest remained at Andersonville, many later to die, inflating the mortality rate still further.

But to single out only Andersonville as the hell hole it was is to forget that there were other prisons where conditions were as bad or worse. For example, at the Northern prison at Elmira, New York, historian James L. Robertson estimates that over 24% of the Southern soldiers, one in four, died there, a figure far exceeding the mortality rate at Andersonville.

To have that many men die in prisoner of war camps is deeply disturbing, and truly represents the seemlier side of the war.

In fact, according to an expert on prisons in the Civil War, William

Hesseltine, when all is counted, over 30,000 Yankees died in Southern prisons, while 26,000 Confederates perished in Northern prisons. That adds up to a 15.5% mortality rate for Yankees in Southern prisons, while 12% of Rebels died in Northern prisons, an abominable figure for both sides, especially considering that the North seemingly had the resources in food, medicine, and physicians that should have offset their figure considerably.

What was life like in Civil War prisons? More particularly, what was prison life like for Kentuckians in Northern prisons? How were Confederate Kentuckians treated considering that these men came from a state that had not seceded from the Union?

One prison that housed Rebel Kentuckians was Camp Douglas in downtown Chicago built on land once owned by Stephen A. Douglas, famed Illinois senator who debated Lincoln just a few years earlier. Fortunately, we have extensive records about life at Camp Douglas from George Levy's 1999 study, *To Die in Chicago*.

In winter, the cold north wind from Lake Michigan whips across the city itself, making heavy clothing a necessity of life that few prisoners were prepared for, especially Southern boys who were not used to such weather. Even the Kentuckians who had experienced winter weather could not have anticipated the bitter cold that grips northern Illinois for much of the year. Many prisoners soon suffered when the weather turned cold, since many desperately needed clothing to protect them. But in large part they did not have adequate protection against the wintry Illinois weather.

Frank Mullen of the Second Confederate Infantry, captured after Chickamauga, was one such typical soldier who was desperate for protective clothing and even resorted to writing to relatives of fellow prisoners, asking them to provide him with clothes:

"I am a strainger to you but am a member of youre son's company.... I am here in prison at Camp Douglas and I would be very thankful to you if you would send me a couple pare of drawers and a couple pare of woolen socks and a blanket for I have none.... I am very bad for clothes and I do not know how long it will be before till we are exchanged."

In fact, the Union commissary general of prisoners, Lt. Colonel William Hoffman, ruled that, "from the 30th of April to the 1st of October neither drawers nor socks will be allowed except to the sick."

Add to that decree by those in command that the prisoners had to supply their own clothing anyway, and men therefore were left to suffer. Adding to the misery, when warm clothes were sent to the prisoners from home, they were often confiscated, because, according to the authorities, the clothing would aid prisoners in escapes.

Needless to say, there was great suffering from the cold for those prisoners in Camp Douglas.

But suffering from the bitter cold was not the extent of the cruelty at Camp Douglas.

Private Curtis R. Burke, Company B, 14th Kentucky Cavalry, who arrived at Camp Douglas in August of 1863, kept a journal of his experiences at the camp in which he describes a device used to punish prisoners known as "Riding the Mule," "The Yanks have fixed a frame near the gate with a scantling across it edge up, and about four feet from the ground, which they make our men ride whenever the men do anything that does not please them." Burke then explains what the punishment is: "Men have sat on it till they fainted and fell off. It is like riding a sharp top fence."

Burke then details when "The Mule" was used in conjunction with other tortures: "If the least sight of water or spit was seen on the floor the order was, come go to the mule or point for grub, which was to stand with the legs perfectly straight, reach over, and touch the ground with the fingers. If the legs were bent in the least, a guard was present with a paddle which he knew how to use." Such punishments were meted out for infractions as minor as talking in the barracks after 8:00 p.m.

One night in a drunken rage, the guards forced the prisoners out of the barracks and ordered them to stand on one foot, while several prisoners were hung upside down and beaten with a belt. Burke notes that "all of the men in one whole barrack was made to stand out awhile and then bare themselves and sit on the snow and ice till they melted through the ground."

Yet in spite of all the cruelties, the Yankees added other miseries to the life of the Southern soldier. The War Department saw fit to reduce the rations given to the prisoners when federal authorities heard rumors about how little the Union soldiers in Southern prisons were given to eat. Burke complains that "it will be three or four days til we draw [rations] again... the men were living on scraps....." Another prisoner recorded that he "saw one poor fellow who had lost his mind for fear of starving to death, and his cries for bread were pitiful in the extreme."

Soon the prisoners, desperate for meat, began eating rats and dogs. W.D. Crump from Company C of the Third Kentucky Cavalry later wrote that the men, "could hardly control their desire for meat and when they could catch rats and cats, they ate them voraciously." One incident illustrates one way this gnawing for food turned. Crump records that, "we were allowed very few visitors, but I recall one man who came to the Camp with a dog following him. The visitor was somehow granted permission to see one of the prisoners, and when he entered the confines the dog came in with him—but he did not leave with him."

Burke records that the dog of Lieutenant Joel A. Fife was lured into the kitchen where it was killed, dressed, and served to prisoners of another barracks as a gesture of goodwill. Burke notes the prisoners "had a rare dish for dinner—they ate the dog and drank the soup."

Prisoner W.D. Henry commented that the usual fare was hardly satisfactory: "There was no more nutritious matter in it than an old dish cloth, for dinner one pint of bean soup and five ounces of bread, this was our living."

It should not be surprising that amid such squalid conditions that included scurvy, resulting from fruits and vegetables being purposely withheld, that men would die. One woman with the best intentions supplied seeds to the prisoners so that they could grow a garden and supply themselves with the necessary vegetables, but the guards ate the harvest. Scurvy got to be so bad that one prisoner notes that "lips were eaten away, jaws became diseased and teeth fell out. If leprosy is any worse than scurvy, may God have mercy on the victim! It was shocking, horrible monstrous, and a disgrace to any people who permitted such conditions to exist."

Among other factors, frigid conditions in the barracks accounted for over 1,091 deaths over a four-month period from November 1864 to February 1865. Levy notes that the death toll "equaled the deaths at Andersonville from February to May 1864."

Out of 26,060 prisoners, 4,009 died, a percentage of over 15 percent dying at the camp, one person out of seven. At Camp Douglas, during the war, there was a report of 70,080 cases of diseases ranging from smallpox, malaria, scurvy, bronchitis, pneumonia, anemia, consumption, and diarrhea. Of those diseases, smallpox accounted for 823 deaths, a figure of 20.5 percent of the total deaths. Levy records that Camp Douglas ranks first in the number of deaths at Northern camps, even though the camp was not the largest prison in the North.

Burke says that at one point, "there were two candles burning all night, and several of the men sat up with the sick flux [diarrhea] patients. The barrack assumes the appearance of a hospital." Later, he notes: "everybody walks light and speaks in whispers on account of the sick." A final insult was that those who did die at Camp Douglas were buried in unmarked graves.

Levy observes that, ironically, many of the soldiers figured their chances of survival were greater on the battlefield than trying to survive at Camp Douglas.

Truly, the Kentucky Confederates suffered mightily during their incarceration at Camp Douglas. And, of course, they were just some amid the many who also suffered there. One prisoner asked, "I wondered what caused all of this fearful mortality…Was it starvation, neglect, and cruelty? God alone knows."

Indeed, it is not clear what caused the legitimate prisoners of war to be treated in such a manner. Some would argue that the North was treating its prisoners the way they did in retaliation for the way the South treated theirs. And there is some truth to that charge. But obviously, that hardly justifies the policy.

Few know about the horrible conditions at Camp Douglas and at other prisoner of war camps in the North and South. More attention has been focused on places like Andersonville. But in order to paint a complete picture of what prisoner of war camps were like in the Civil War, the conditions at Camp Douglas deserve attention, attention that for too long has been lacking.

Historian Hesseltine reminds us that "the atrocities of prison camps were only phases of the greater atrocity of war itself."

Curiously, the men who survived Camp Douglas, along with those who survived other prison camps during the war, often recounted their tales of woe and their experiences to the succeeding generation. Yet somehow those accounts have been largely forgotten. Ultimately, though, if we are to understand the war in its fullest, we must fill in the details of this horrendous picture of life at the prisoner of war camps North and South and learn the sad lessons of history of man's inhumanity to man.

Religion in the Civil War and the Good Parson Wynne's Dilemma

The old cliché is "that there are no atheists in a foxhole." It seems that in battle men and women naturally turn to their God for comfort and strength.

The thinking is that God will offer them succor in their most trying times. So soldiers often facing the prospect of an impending death turn to some higher power to explain the chaos of battle and to be assured of the promise of life after death.

The Civil War was no exception.

The deeply religious Confederate General T.J. "Stonewall" Jackson was a bit fatalistic about it all, once telling a fellow general that, "my religious belief teaches me to feel as safe in battle as in bed. God has fixed the time for my death. I do not concern myself about that, but to be always ready, no matter when it may overtake me," and then added, "That is the way all men should live, and then all would be equally brave."

But both sides also thought that theirs was the just cause, that God was on their side.

General Robert E. Lee, himself a devoted Christian, said that, "God is our only refuge and our strength...Let us confess our many sins, and beseech him to give us higher courage, a purer patriotism and more determined will: that he will convert the hearts of our enemies...."

According to Andrew Coopersmith, writing in the magazine *North and South*, "in the religious culture that prevailed in the nineteenth-century South, nothing that happened in life was accidental or trivial. Events unfolded by the will of God; all things contributed to His grand and unknowable plan for humankind. Accordingly, when the war erupted in 1861, it was a point of faith among Southerners that the creation of the Confederacy was part of God's handiwork." Following that line of logic, then, the South, "had broken free from the Union because God wanted it that way."

When the war was not going well, and defeats in battle tended to curb religious zeal, the South thought that, "they had to be reminded that misfortunes befall people not because God has abandoned them, but because they have behaved sinfully and deserved punishment." But, all in all, they must remember, God was with them.

Curiously, Lois Davis of Dracut, Massachusetts in writing to her son avowed that God was not on the side of the Confederates, but rather argued that God was on the side of the Union: "Yours is a holy cause and may the God of battle watch over and protect you is my constant prayer."

Someone no less than Admiral David G. Farragut said, "As I believe God is on our side, I believe He will sooner or later give us victory."

President Abraham Lincoln mused that "both [sides] read the same Bible and pray to the same God; and each invokes His aid against the other," but he added, "It may seem strange that any men should dare to ask a just God's assistance in wringing their bread from the sweat of other men's faces; but let us not judge that we be not judged."

And, closer to home, one abolitionist noted that, "Mr. Lincoln would like to have God on his side, but he must have Kentucky."

But there were other less optimistic views about God working in the great conflict.

J.M. Davis, a Confederate soldier facing Union General William Tecumseh Sherman and his troops as they made their way across Georgia: "It seems like the Lord has turned his face from us and left us to work out our own destruction."

The crusty old General Sherman pooh-poohed the whole idea that God was even needed in the roar of war: "Crackers and oats are more necessary to my army than any moral or religious authority."

But the people in charge in Richmond and Washington didn't feel that way; they realized the place of spiritual care in soldiers' lives and set about to appoint chaplains to minister to the soldiers.

According to historian John Melnick, at one time, the Union side had 1,079 chaplains on duty: 930 regimental chaplains, 117 hospital chaplains, and 32 post chaplains. These chaplains were, at first, ordained men of the cloth who assumed officer's rank and a handsome pay of $100 a month. According to Charles White, writing on the role of chaplains in the war, the administration, meeting stiff opposition by Jewish leaders, later changed the policy to allow representatives of any organized religion to serve as chaplains.

Both White and Melnick say that the Confederates had between 600-1,000 Methodist, Presbyterian, Episcopal, Baptist, and Roman Catholics to serve as ministers to the troops.

A chaplain in typical regalia. Library of Congress photo.

Faith in the Fight: Civil War Chaplains records that a total of 3,694 men and one woman served as chaplains on both sides.

White notes that wherever troops gathered there were crude constructions to serve as altars. Sticks, logs, boards and even cracker boxes served as primitive chapels and churches to the spiritually hungry.

One of the most famous incidents that symbolized the importance of these men of God occurred at the Battle of Gettysburg when Father William Corby, serving as chaplain to the Irish Brigade, asked the colonel in charge for permission to address his flock. As Melnick tells it, Father Corby "donned his purple stole, mounted a nearby rock, extended his hand, and pronounced brief words of absolution over the soldiers."

Melnick continues: "Witnesses later reported that every man in sight, Catholic, other faith, and atheist, dropped to his knees in unison as Father Corby made the Sign of the Cross."

As *The Encyclopedia of Civil War Usage* notes, Federal chaplains typically dressed in a black frock coat, plain black pants, and a black felt hat to mark them as noncombatants.

But there is still another side to the spiritual ministering by these Men of the Cloth.

The nineteenth century was also the time of strait-laced hellfire and damnation preaching, when soldiers were reminded that unless they gave up their besmirched and evil ways they were headed for hell. According to White, to remind soldiers of their precarious position with their Maker, along with Bibles, soldiers got copies of tracts with such foreboding titles as, "A Mother's Parting Words to Her Soldier Boy," "Are You Ready to Die," and "You Are Soon to Be Damned." Many saw religion as the practice of strictly obeying God's laws to prepare for either salvation or damnation.

But sometimes these men of the cloth found themselves presented with some sticky moral decisions.

In *The Civil War Reminiscences of General Basil W. Duke, C.S.A*, the memoirs of General John Hunt Morgan's second in command and brother-in-law, Duke tells a humorous story about a man he calls Parson Wynne. Not much is known about the reverend except that he was a strict, by-the-book individual, what Duke calls "an excellent soldier, but a pious and good man, who justly exercised a great influence over his comrades."

But Duke also notes that Parson Wynne was "rather irritable and extremely stubborn in the maintenance and assertion of his opinions."

Duke tells us that the good parson was often paired with another Morgan soldier, Dan Ray, to conduct secret missions in Kentucky. It seems that Ray saw himself as appointed to "stir up the parson" and enjoyed it immensely, for Parson Wynne was easily excitable, especially about matters of morality and religion.

One day, on a mission in southern Kentucky, as Duke tells it, Ray and Wynne began to discuss the practice of impressing horses for use by the cavalry. Impressing, or "pressing" as it was commonly called, referred to soldiers' taking horses for their own use from local farmers and not often paying for them. Farmers were sometimes "paid" in useless Confederate scrip, worthless in exchange for hard cash.

The parson, of course, saw impressing horses as absolute stealing, a clear violation of God's laws. Or as Duke says, "it could not be defended or excused for any reason." Duke goes on to say that Parson Wynne, "prayed daily that his comrades might be forgiven for the sin, but intimated in strong terms that he didn't believe they would be." Denouncing the practice broadly, he believed that impressing horses was a "national crime" that would "bring about the fall of the Confederacy."

The next day the good reverend stopped at a blacksmith's shop to get a horse shod, but the blacksmith carelessly pricked one of the horse's hooves enough that later in the day the horse turned up lame.

The parson was caught in a dilemma: should they go all the way back to the blacksmith to get another horse, or should they continue on with the injured horse until they could get another mount?

At about that same time, an obviously wealthy man came riding down the road with what Duke describes as "a remarkably fine horse." As Duke says, at that point, "the parson longed, looked, and let go all his scruples. He felt it was predestined that he should have the horse."

"That's a mighty likely looking horse you're riding, sir—a mighty likely animal," the parson said to the rich man.

"Yes," he's a right peart nag."

"Sound, too, ain't he? Nothing the matter with him?" Parson Wynne asked.

"Well, stranger, he's sound from his eyes to his hocks. Thar ain't a soft spot in him."

At this time, Parson Wynne pointed to his own horse: "This is a good chunk of a horse, too." and proceeded to praise his horse, regaling the unfortunate listener with the bloodline and qualities of the lame animal.

"But a fool blacksmith pricked him this morning," the parson pleaded.

"Pull off his shoes and let him stand in the grass," the wealthy man suggested.

"I haven't the time, I am engaged in public service and must get on rapidly, so I am compelled to ask _you_ to swap horses," the parson explained. "You have leisure and seem to be an intelligent man, and you can doctor the horse."

The man shot back: "The hell you say! Well, stranger, you're the drunkest man to hide it so well I ever see!"

"Don't use profane language in my presence!" the parson retorted, and added that the man was getting the "best of the trade," as he effected a trade of horses and saddles, and punctuated the command with "forced obedience by the production of an army Colt."

Soon Parson Wynne and Dan Ray were back on the trail with the good reverend sitting proudly on a new horse.

Ray, of course, could not let all of this go. "Parson, I have been pondering over what you said yesterday about horse-pressing, and I've about concluded you were right. I am satisfied that it can't be defended, and —"

"Dan Ray," the parson interrupted, "I don't care to hear you discuss a matter you can't understand. Your mind hasn't been trained to draw nice distinctions. That matter awhile back wasn't properly a case of horse-pressing at all. It was a compulsory trade, rendered necessary by the unsettled condition of the country and the times, and because the laws regulating the making and enforcement of contracts are rather silent right now. I could demonstrate this without the slightest difficulty to any man accustomed to logical discussion; but if you ever allude to it again, I'll hang in your wool!"

It seems in the popular parlance of today, the good Parson Wynne was "theologically challenged."

The Case of Dr. Mary Edwards Walker: What Really Happened in That Louisville Civil War Prison?

On July 31, 1864, in Civil War Louisville, Kentucky, a city deeply divided over the question of secession, and, as a result, host to a large contingency of Union soldiers, a group of bedraggled, angry, and bewildered women, children, and a few men from rural Georgia straggled into the city to begin their time as prisoners of war, a stay that would last until the end of the war, when on April 21, 1865, the last few prisoners were released and wandered back home.

While part of their group of 400 were sent north of the Ohio River to work in mills in places like Indianapolis and the Cannelton, Indiana Cotton Mill, a facility down river from Louisville some 70-80 miles, most of the unfortunate ladies and their offspring ended up in Louisville at a dreadful facility called the Louisville Female Military Prison, on Broadway between Twelfth and Thirteenth Street.

During their nearly nine-month stay in the Falls City, the women and children's health needs were attended to by Dr. Mary Edwards Walker, a native upstate New Yorker with a wide-spread reputation as a social revolutionary who often displayed shocking eccentricities for her time, like refusing to wear the dresses of the era, balking adamantly at saying wedding vows that included words like "love, honor, and obey," and declining then to assume her husband's last name, whom she later divorced. In addition, she campaigned for causes like women suffrage and temperance, and railed against tight-fitting women's clothing and the use of tobacco. Lincoln's Secretary of War, Edwin M. Stanton, summed her up quite well: "She lived a life of determined unconventionality."

What happened between this group of grumbling Georgians and

Dr. Walker is the subject of great and lengthy debate. One side argues that Dr. Walker performed admirable service for the women and children while they were in Louisville, improving their lot and caring for them when others wouldn't; in other words, she was a tender and devoted Angel of Mercy in tough times.

But the other side casts Dr. Walker as a veritable she-devil, a cruel, spiteful, vengeful, and power-hungry man-hating machine who should have been severely censured instead of being the first woman to be awarded the Congressional Medal of Honor on November 11, 1865, by President Andrew Johnson, an honor revoked in 1917, perhaps, in part for her reputation as a social activist, but restored posthumously on June 10, 1977 by President Jimmy Carter.

The story that leads to the considerable controversy began in Roswell, Georgia, where the mighty army of Union General William Tecumseh Sherman marched through the South to the sea at Savannah, sowing destruction and despair in its path, an army that Sherman vowed would, "make old and young, rich and poor, feel the hard hand of war."

A portion of that massive movement of men was the Second Division of the Army of the Cumberland, a cavalry unit that descended upon the little Georgia town only to discover three factories: one woolen works, a cotton rope installation, and a massive cotton factory that produced material for the Confederate war effort. While at first the owners of the factories insisted that the factories were operating under French auspices, the Union troops soon found ample evidence in the form of Confederate uniforms that the operation was no French millinery.

In command of the unit that located the mills was native Kentuckian Brigadier Kenner Garrard, born in Bourbon County, the grandson of Kentucky's second governor, a 1851 graduate of West Point, who had served, before the war, under both Confederate Generals Albert Sidney Johnston and Robert E. Lee.

On July 6, 1864, Garrard quickly wrote Sherman and detailed what he had found.

When he learned about the factories, the next day, Sherman delivered a stern order to Garrard: "Their utter destruction is right and meets my entire approval, and to make the matter complete you will arrest the owners and employees and send them, under guard, charged with treason, to Marietta."

Three days later, after some Rebel resistance from troops in the area, the factories were ablaze, and six days later the ragtag group of women, men, and children had made it to Marietta, Georgia, and then on to Nashville by train, arriving there on July 20th.

As historian Michael Hitt observes, when the hot and tired and dusty group of women and children finally made it to Louisville that last day of July, their sympathizers weren't just those favoring the Confederate cause. The Harrisburg, Pennsylvania newspaper, the *Patriot and Union*, said of Sherman: "General Sherman has shown on two or three occasions that [his] ability as a military commander is quite compatible with something not far removed from imbecility in respect to civil matters."

On August 9th, however, the famous editor of the *Louisville Daily Journal*, George Prentice, defended Sherman's action, but mistakenly thought that the woman and children had "importuned General Sherman to send them where [the women] could find work and security," calling Sherman's move an "exercise of an enlarged and generous spirit of humanity...," but as Hitt points out, Sherman had in actuality "charged [the women] with treason." They were, in fact, not looking for jobs, but, rather, they were prisoners of war and charged with treason.

Yet by August 24th, Prentice published a more sympathetic story, decrying the conditions of the women's prison, but noting that "a few noble-hearted ladies of the city have been doing what they could from day to day, and the surgeon of the prison, Dr. [E.O.] Brown, has visited them as constantly as his other duties would permit. There are children of every age, some so attenuated as to be living skeletons, perishing from want of care."

Perhaps the authorities in Washington received word of the need for changes in the care of the women and children prisoners in Louisville, for on September 22nd, under orders from Assistant Surgeon General, Joseph B. Brown, Dr. Mary Edwards Walker, who had served with other military commanders during the war, and had for a time been a prisoner of war herself, was directed to "report in person, without delay for duty with prisoners" in Louisville.

Underscoring the plight of the prisoners, the next day, the *Louisville Daily Journal* ran another story on the condition of the women and children, reporting that "nine-tenths are prostrate with disease. Several deaths have occurred during this week...and the physician in charge says immediate relief must be given, or all will die. They must be removed to other quarters, with what little they have now being rotten with filth and vermin."

To make matters even worse, General Sherman received a message from Union Major General J.M. Schofield, written October 3rd, alleging that certain officers released prisoners after they made exorbitant payments to military personnel in Louisville, in addition to other forms of official misconduct. Schofield wrote: "The charges relative to corruption in the release of prisoners involve the official character of Brevet-Major-General Stephen Gano Burbridge...," a name already widely reviled in Kentucky for what many Kentuckians saw as high-handed tactics and tyrannical rule.

Dr. Mary Edwards Walker: Early feminist and physician who served in the war.

A year later, and after Burbridge had been relieved of command in January of 1865, Burbridge replied that the problems with corruption in Louisville stemmed from two men: Captain Stephen Jones and Lieutenant Colonel J.H. Hammond, who were both "rabid McClellan men, and [were] using their influence and position against me, in my endeavor to carry the state for Mr. Lincoln." But by January 15, 1865, trouble of another type was brewing in the ladies' prison, for Dr. Walker was replying to accusations from the post commandant after a disturbance in the female prison. The inmates cited the cause to be the doctor's mistreatment of the inmates, a charge the post commandant, presumably Major General John Palmer, agreed with. In bitter words, calling his accusations "a gross injustice," in her letter, Walker explained in some detail that the women were upset with her because she would "not allow rebel songs and disloyal talk..., or familiarity between the guards, male cooks and prisoners." Walker went on to say that she "exacted cleanliness," did not permit "prisoners to abuse each other...," "and did not allow them to "neglect their small children..., pass letters without examining them, and ...permit talk [she could] not hear."

She concluded her note to the commandant with stinging sarcasm: "Give them their filth, unrestrained disloyalty and immorality and it would be satisfactory times with them. I am an eyesore to them, and they want men cooks again, and a man Doctor."

One of her biographers, Dale L. Walker (no kin), supports Dr. Walker's contention that she did much good in Louisville. He says, for example, that she gave the lady prisoners "better diets–coffee, soups, fresh beef, vegetables. She demanded cleanliness; replaced male cooks with females to improve the menus; tolerated 'no Rebel songs or disloyal talk,' and no profanity." In addition, "she wrote letters on behalf of certain prisoners, especially teenage girls, urging that they be freed and sent home; she treated their illnesses, and...earned the praise of her orderlies and the prison's medical director, Dr. Edward Phelps," who "wrote a glowing report" about her "'active, energetic, and persevering spirit.'"

But the women in the prison portrayed another quite different version of Dr. Walker. Frances Thomas Howard's *In and Out of the Lines*, subtitled *An Accurate Account of Incidents during the Occupation of Georgia by Federal Troops*, written in 1905, based on the memories of those that experienced imprisonment in Louisville, begins her description of Dr. Walker by quoting former prisoner Rose McDonald's impression of the physician: "If ever a fiend in human guise walked this earth it did it in that woman's body. Her character was a combination of brutality, malice, and cowardice."

According to the prisoners, Dr. Walker displayed conduct so cruel and so impertinent that the hapless prisoners had no other choice, but to threaten some sort of violence against her to deal with her mistreatment of them.

One incident involved a broom. Receiving payment from sewing on stripes on the uniform of a guard, the prisoner Rose McDonald bought a broom to sweep her living area. Later, Dr. Walker asked to borrow the broom, promising to quickly return it. But Dr. Walker failed to bring it back, even when Ms. McDonald repeatedly asked for it. At the advice of a fellow inmate, Ms. McDonald saw the broom in another room and quickly seized it, reasoning that it was indeed hers and she had a right to it. When Dr. Walker learned that Ms. McDonald had the broom, she severely chastised Ms. McDonald for taking what the physician called "the prison's broom."

Ms. McDonald, though, insisted that it was indeed _her_ broom, at which point Dr. Walker gave her a hard slap across the face.

Ms. McDonald, then, picked up a handy iron poker and vowed to kill the doctor if she ever touched her again, a remark that landed Ms. McDonald an extended stay in the dark dungeon, a dank and bitter cold room below the floor.

Another time, Dr. Walker supposedly saw a small child at the top of the stairs, munching on a piece of bread, and yelled out at the baby, "Get out of my way, you little brat!" and kicked the child down the flight of stairs.

Prisoners also accused the doctor of stealing their Christmas dinner supplied by the kind ladies of Louisville, and sending two women to the dungeon that same day for waving at Confederate prisoners passing by.

Still another time, Dr. Walker was said to have set fire to a nearby building, with billows of heavy smoke quickly engulfing the prison, and when the women, fearing for their very lives, begged to be evacuated, she hid the keys from the guards.

What is the truth about Dr. Mary Edwards Walker? Was she the "fiend" that the ladies from Georgia saw her as? Or was she an "Angel of Mercy" who served her patients well, but remained the victim of prejudice against her for her station as a woman?

A recent trend in research, especially by some Southern historians on the Civil War, is to re-evaluate the treatment the South received at the hands of their Yankee conquerors. More and more books and articles explore what General William Tecumseh Sherman and his army did while they marched to the sea. Sherman, certainly, vowed "to make Georgia howl," which surely invites many to demonize "Uncle Billy" and his tactics. But did that attitude apply to all Southerners like the ladies in the Louisville prison?

In other words, was Dr. Mary Edwards Walker a symbolic part of Sherman's plans? Or, rather, is the doctor just a victim of her own eccentricities?

It is difficult to say.

But even today, nearly 150 years after the war, many people in Georgia think they know the answers to those questions.

Day to Day in the Orphan Brigade

The Orphan Brigade is one of the most interesting and tenacious bunch of soldiers the Commonwealth ever produced. Officially known as the First Kentucky Brigade of the Confederate Army, they began with 3,000 men and ended the Civil War with only about 500.

They fought proudly at places like Shiloh, Stone's River, Corinth, Baton Rouge, Vicksburg, Chickamauga, and Missionary Ridge, and throughout the Atlanta campaign. They were, in fact, among the last Confederate soldiers in the East to surrender.

Their unmatched bravery and devoted camaraderie are legendary among Civil War historians.

But what about their everyday life? What was it like? What did they do with their time? How did they relate to each other? What was battle like for the individual soldier?

Fortunately, three people from the Orphan Brigade published books after the war. These are not the journals of officers, but the records of ordinary, everyday soldiers who wanted to share their stories with family, friends, and ultimately the world. At times the spelling, punctuation can prove challenging to the modern reader, but these idiosyncrasies are part of the charm of their records.

The first one is Conrad Wise Chapman's memoir called *Ten Months in The Orphan Brigade*, edited by Ben Bassham.

Chapman was the son of John Gadsby Chapman, the artist who painted The Baptism of Pocahontas for the Capitol Rotunda in Washington, D.C. Both the elder and the son were living in Italy at the time of the outbreak of the Civil War. Ultimately, young Conrad joined the Paducah Company of the brigade in Bowling Green, Kentucky.

Although the time Chapman spent with the Orphan Brigade was short, his record of his adventures is no less interesting. It was the high point of his life, for not only did he use words to tell his story, but he also sketched his companions in pencil in a few surviving drawings (unfortunately, most were lost).

Of his experiences with the Orphan Brigade, he concluded: "My character was formed in the armies of the South [and] for better or worse I must abide by it."

This first incident records how young some of Chapman's fellow soldiers were, and a neat trick they used to keep one of the young ones in the brigade:

> Otto F. Rosencrantz and Bob Beard were my two best friends in the Co., both messmates. Rosencrantz was a boy 13 or fourteen years old, the youngest soldier in the Co.–At the beginning of the war he was at school and ran away from his father who was a brother of [a] Yankey General and shared his ultra radical opinions–He was anxious to get his runaway boy back again, and begged, threatened and tryed to persuade him to return, and finally sent a substitute for him, with a request to the Col of the regiment to start his son back to Paducah. The sharp little fellow got the substitute sworn in and thanked his father for sending [another] soldier to the Confederacy.

But there were also "ordinary days," days when the soldiers gathered together to forget what Dr. Thomas Clark, the late Kentucky Historian Laureate, termed "the roar of war":

> While poker seven up and Yucka were going on, and confederate notes and silver went the rounds and fell to the most lucky and some times to the most skillful in the art of taking in his adversary, a few of us recounted what little experience we had had in life before joining the army, a gay song, or ritch story enlivened the hours as they passed, Leon would get out his violin and play for us and when he did and I could shut out from around me the scene, of a boisterous camp and listen and forget where I was, I would dream over dreams that I thought a soldiers life had hardened me against forever–I would forget the reality of the drill next morning, my turn on guard, and think of a life such if I had had a chance such as many have had, I came back to my stumpy black pipe

again which had gone out while my thoughts traveled many a mile and brushed a way a tear which none had seen, and tried to laugh at myself for my foolishness. It is strange that through life music always has a great effect on me, and I have not the power of repeating a single tune–I shall never forget when after long persuasion Leon undertook to put an old camp fiddle in tune, and the echoes he woke up in the forest that night. He was an accomplished musician–We grew to be strong friends.

What strikes readers about this passage is not just the record Chapman gives of everyday life, but also, in spite of the odd spellings and punctuation, the beautiful writing, the keen eye for detail and the ever-present reminder that war was always in the back of their minds, even when they seemed to be doing something else.

And then there was always sleeping: How? Where? When? How long? Those were obvious and very important questions to a soldier.

In the winter, sleeping on the cold or frozen dirt can be a teeth-chattering experience. With so few blankets and with no source of heat other than the human body, how do you keep warm?

In situations like these, the common practice in Civil War circles was spooning (sleeping cuddled against another soldier also facing forward).

In one place Chapman talks about finding a place to sleep and spooning:

> Chap where shall we make our bed, was Rosencranz first question on reaching camp and our blankets were put down to secure the place, fellows claimed any spot they could sellect after leaving their hat or canteen to mark the spot, while other[s] presume to lay claims to spots they had decided on without any such mark of possession–It may seem strange that men should be so childish about a place to sleep on, but amongst soldiers some soon get to be selfish, and would rather have a partner grumbling at the uneven ground and protruding stump and roots under his blanket, than have to sleep under such difficulties one's self–Rosencranz and I each had a blanket and any third one of the party who would join us, we would place two blankets down to sleep on to keep out the wet, and lying spoon fashion close together and [another] to cover with keep warm all night. It was always preferable to sleep in the middle for you were then sure of having your portion of the blanket undisputed.

But, of course, there was always the terror of battle. While many try to make sense out of the often confusing military tactics used in battle (this army attacks the enemy's left flank, for example), ultimately a military battle is a bewildering experience to describe in logical, sequential, cause and effect terms. But Chapman's description captures much of this horror and confusion:

> We advanced over broken and tangled ground [.] [T]rees had been cut down across our path by both the axx and cannon—My hat was caught by a twig as we moved on, but it was no time to look back on—on and on we moved keeping our line as best we could. Double quick boys, we will soon be on them, and a few fellows fell in our rear as we advanced and saw the blue coats of the enemy looming in the distance—Our officer cautioned us to aim low and take deliberate aim—We came to a halt where we had good cover—and soon the blue bellys commenced to show themselves more clearly—and the order was given to commence firing—Bang bang and the work commenced—I had little time to look about but there were gallant things done on all sides, fellows braving the whole thing, [m]any going in front of the line, placing a tree between them and the main line—But it was load and shoot all the time, fellows fell on all sides of me and a thought crossed my mind that the hand of death might be hovering close to me at the time—For a soldier to describe a battle, it is impossible to do so for he never sees but the incidents

The Orphan Brigade at a post-war reunion. Courtesy of the Kentucky Historical Society.

immediately near him and even those through a mist as it were of powder and excitement. I remember the Colonel with his wounded arm pointing to the front, the cartridges beginning to give out of my box, and the feeling that I was about to fire my last when, suddenly as I was ramming it down, I felt as if a hot cannon ball had struck me on the head, and remember nothing more as I must have fainted that very moment from loss of blood. When I came to I found my gun gone and the fellows around me saying it was no use taking him off the field he has gone up at the spout—Look at his head—I had not the courage to open my eyes, my first movement was to feel if I still lived—if such a sensation can be understood. The terrible feeling of that moment I shall never forget–Every action of my life seemed written before me—When I opened my eyes the battle was still going on, and many had bit the dust like myself—I put my hand to my head where I remember having been struck for I felt no pain—and my hand when I looked at it told a fearful story and felt the warm blood running down my back in a perfect stream—I looked for the man I had called on to help me before the battle, but he was near a tree and perhaps wounded also for when I beckoned to him he took no notice, so I had to crawl as best I could to a tree close by, after having made several vain efforts to rise, I put the tree between me and the foe for the battle still raged all around. While drooping in this way my head leaning against the tree, I noticed a little violet looking up to me from under the trampled grass, and a thought of past scenes of a different nature passed through my mind as I plucked it and put it in my sketchbook next to my bosom. It is strange how one little thing in Gods creation can turn ones mind from scenes such as I was then surrounded by—That little flower I carefully kept and pressed in my journal as the only trophy I took from the fire of battle.

Others recorded their experiences in the Orphan Brigade, too.

One of them was John S. Jackman, whose editor, William Davis, describes his diary as "the longest, most informative, and most unvarnished account available of service in the famed 'Orphan Brigade.'"

Jackman is an able recorder of the plight of the Confederate soldier to find something to eat; the daily allotment of corn meal and salt pork left most Rebels still hungry.

Jackman, for example, tells of an unique way the boys caught some fish:

> We had a good place to bathe, in Pearl river. The boys caught a great many fish out of the lake and river. One way of catching them was rather novel: Two men would go into the lake, when the water was not very deep, and hold a blanket spread out, down close to the water, then others would commence lashing the water about, making it muddy, and the fish would commence skipping above the surface of the lake and fall on the blanket, thus being caught by hundreds.

And Jackman also takes a few moments in his journal to describe what life was like in the bleak, gray winters. But surprisingly, he sees another side to that season:

> Camp life is not so horrible as one might suppose. The "old heroes of an hundred battles" assemble around the roaring log fires, kindled on their earthen hearths, some to talk of the gay times they will have "when this cruel war is over," to recount their adventures and hardships in former campaigns, and to speculate on those to be made in the future; and, not seldom, to talk of their faraway homes, many of which are in the lines of the enemy; others again read their bibles by the light of a blazing pine-knot—"soldier's candles"—while many seek amusement in the mysteries of "seven-up," "poker," and other games. Thus are the long winter evenings [wiled] away. When wearied, they retire to their rough couches, perhaps to wander in sweet dreams to their faraway homes, and are surrounded by loved ones. Ah! many can visit their homes only in dreams. They have been driven back, step by step, dying their native soil with their blood—driven into exile. What a proud day it will be to these exiled-veterans, when the foe is hurled back from our borders, and they can once again cross their threshholds in reality, to meet the dear ones from whom they have been separated so long.

Perhaps the most remarkable passages from the journals of soldiers from the Orphan Brigade comes from the memoirs of Johnny Green, who describes one of the several times he escaped the cold hand of death. As A.D. Kirwan, who edited Green's remarkable journal, notes, "Green was a sensitive observer who had a flair for descriptive writing." Green tells his story this way:

> We arrived at a point where our line was hard pressed, we were ordered to charge and went in with a yell, we drove the yankees before us and followed them across an open field

through one of their camps. One yankee who stood his ground firing from behind one of their tents had drawn a bead on Captain Price Newman who was in hot pursuit at the head of his company. I fired at Mr. Yank as I advanced but missed him; he fired at Capt Newman not fifteen feet distant, who fell headlong. I rushed for a clump of bushes to take shelter long enough to reload and just as I had loaded and was raising my gun to fire I fell from a bullit which struck me just over the heart. I felt sure it had gone clear through me and it flashed through my mind that I would live until the arterial blood started back to my heart, when I would drop dead, as I had once seen a deer do which my father shot through the heart. I rose to my knees, took a hurried aim and fired at a clump of the enemy. By this time I was surprised to find that I was still alive. I felt my breast to learn the extent of my wound when I found one piece of the bullit laying against my skin inside my clothes just over my heart. The ball had passed through the stock of my gun, split on the iron ramrod of my gun, and the other piece had passed through my jacket and burried itself in a little testament in my jacket pocket. The force of the blow knocked me down but nothing more serious had befallen me.

Obviously, much more can be learned from these three men's record of the service with the storied group of men called the Orphan Brigade.

But these vivid vignettes possibly give those interested in the Civil War a view of this unique unit of men not readily available in the long annals of war. Ordinarily, the stories of armed conflict often highlight the massive movements of whole armies, but these diaries help later generations understand what everyday life was like and how battle felt to individual soldiers.

For even now, their words speak to us.

Loreta Velazquez as Lt. Harry T. Burford, C.S.A.: A Kentucky Connection

Like all wars, the Civil War is thought of as a man's war. Men decided to go to war. Men enlisted and were drafted to fight. Men did the fighting. And men decided when to lay down their arms.

But that is not completely true.

According to DeAnne Blanton, writing from The United States National Archives and Records Administration, a "little less than four hundred" women served in the Union army, and some two hundred and fifty served for the South, a total of 750 women managed to enlist as men in the War between the States.

But for reasons not entirely clear, the United States government didn't want to admit that women actually served in the Union army.

In October of 1909, General F.C. Ainsworth, the Adjutant General of the United States, in answer to a query by historian Ida Tarbel about women serving in combat roles in the Civil War, concluded that "no official record has been found in the War Department showing specifically that any woman was ever enlisted in the military service of the United States as a member of any organization of the Regular or Volunteer Army at any time during the period of the civil war. It is possible, however, that there may have been a few instances of women having served as soldiers for a short time without their sex having been detected, but no record of such cases is known to exist in the official files."

Whether or not Ainsworth was reluctant in the tenor of the times to admit that "the weaker sex" could have fought along side men in what most historians call "the first modern war" is, of course, open to speculation. But as Blanton points out, Ainsworth's reply was "untrue," for the "compiled military service records for the participants of the Civil War, both Union and Confederate,...prove the point that the army did have documentation of the service of women soldiers."

The Union soldiers included Mary Burns from a Michigan regiment, Frances Clalin from Missouri, Catherine E. Davidson from the Twenty-eighth Ohio, Sara Emma Edmonds from the Second Michigan, Ellen Goodridge and Sara Collins from Wisconsin, Nelly Graves from the Twenty-fourth New Jersey, Fanny Wilson from the Third Illinois Cavalry, Jennie Hodges of the Ninety-fifth Illinois, Ida Remington from the Eleventh New York Militia, who fought at Antietam, and Mary Wise from an Indiana regiment, just to name a few. In 1934, near the Shiloh battlefield, an unearthed grave of nine Union soldiers included the bones of one woman.

The Confederate soldiers listed Mary and Molly Bell, who served under General Jubal Early; and Margaret Henry, Mary Wright, and Malinda Blalock as women who served the Confederate cause. According to Blanton, one body found after Gettysburg suggested that one Rebel part of Pickett's charge was indeed a woman.

In those Victorian days of extreme personal modesty, it was possible for a woman to assume the identity of a man. Blanton notes, for example, that "a woman soldier would not call undue attention to herself if she acted modestly, trekked to the woods to answer the call of nature and attend to other personal matters, or left camp before dawn to privately bathe in a nearby stream." Blanton also says that enlistment physical exams were "usually farcical," with only obvious physical limitations like deafness, poor eyesight, or loss of limb disqualifying an applicant.

Perhaps the most interesting and controversial woman soldier to serve as a man in the war, Loreta Janeta Velazquez, posing as Lieutenant Harry T. Buford, had a Kentucky connection.

In 1876, Velazquez published her memoirs, including her life as a Civil War soldier, with the contentious title of *The Woman in Battle*, which seemed to be an outright challenge to the Victorian norms of the day that couldn't fathom a woman fighting in so many major battles and providing so much service to the Confederacy.

Sylvia D. Hoffert, writing in *Civil War Times* magazine notes that among those who were the most outraged was former Confederate General Jubal Early, who earned lasting fame as a raider who nearly made it to Washington, D.C. Early said flatly that "the writer of that book, whether man or woman, had never had the adventures therein narrated." Early went on: "She could not be what she pretended to be" and then listed "several inconsistencies, absurdities, and impossibilities" in the book.

Velazquez later wrote to Early to defend herself. She argued that her impression of the war naturally differed from his impression of the war because she had a totally different perspective as a soldier: "I do not pretend to know even one truth that transpired upon any one battlefield I served upon. I only endeavor to give the most important facts that came under my immediate observation." She then listed a Who's Who of Southern governmental officials, including former Vice President of the Confederacy Alexander H. Stephens of Georgia, former governor of Tennessee John C. Brown, and Congressman John M. Glover of Missouri as references to her character.

Was Velazquez telling the truth about her many exploits posing as a man in the Confederate army?

Her biography in the authoritative *American National Biography* concludes that "recent research into the details of her narrative... suggests that although there is some contradiction and inconsistency in her text–which she claimed to have written without notes–enough remains that can be corroborated to suggest that some version of the truth is retold...."

To her credit, the *Official Records of the Union and Confederate Armies* does list Miss Alice Williams, one of Velazquez's many aliases, this time as a double-agent for the South, and says that she was "commissioned in the rebel army as a lieutenant under the name of Buford," exactly the name she used as a male Rebel soldier.

Newspapers in Louisville, New Orleans, Jackson, Mississippi, and Richmond published details to give credence to her story, too

There seems to be little doubt that she did pose as a man called Lieutenant Harry T. Buford and in the main her adventures are historically accurate, while most readers will find portions of her autobiography embellished in places for willing nineteenth century readers anxious to read her story. In 2003, Jesse Aleman, the editor of the reprint of her of book probably says it best: *"The Woman in Battle* is undeniably part pulp fiction, but it is not necessarily inauthentic."

Velazquez was born in Havana, Cuba in 1842 of a Spanish father and a French American mother; the young Velazquez eventually ended up in New Orleans to complete her formal education. As a young girl, she was fascinated by the French military leader, Joan of Arc. As she says: "From my early childhood, Joan of Arc was my favorite heroine; and many a time has my soul burned with an overwhelming desire to emulate her deeds of valor, and to make for myself a name which like hers, would be enrolled in letters of gold among the woman who had the courage to fight like men–ay, better than most men–for a great cause, for friends, and for father-land."

Early in the book, she admits that she "was especially haunted with the idea of being a man; and the more I thought upon the subject, the more I was disposed to murmur at Providence for having created me a woman."

Married to an unnamed army officer, when the Civil War broke out, her husband threw his allegiance to the Southern cause and she begged him to let her sign up, too, but he objected and forbade her to volunteer dressed as a man. After he left, she sought a tailor to make her a Confederate lieutenant's uniform, fashioned devices to disguise her gender, including a glued on mustache, and headed for backwoods Arkansas where she recruited a regiment, in spite of the romantic intentions of a young lady, and promptly delivered them to her surprised husband stationed in Pensacola, Florida. She is unexpectedly widowed when her husband is killed when a carbine explodes in his hands.

From then on, she became an itinerant soldier, moving from one place to another on both the eastern and western theaters of war in search of combat action. At first, she said "the sensations of a soldier in the thick of a fight baffle description; and as his hopes rise or sink with the ebb and flow of battle, as he sees comrades falling about him dead and wounded, hears the sharp hiss of the bullets, the shrieking of each other, there is a positive enjoyment in the deadly perils of the occasion that nothing can equal," an attitude that changed dramatically as the war wears on.

She fought as Lieutenant Buford at Bull Run and Ball's Bluff, assumed her natural gender and worked as a spy in Washington, and met United States Secretary of War, Salmon P. Cameron, and President Abraham Lincoln, whom she described as "not what I would call an ugly man, for he had a pleasant, kindly face, and a pleasantly familiar manner, that puts one at ease with him immediately," but her

Loreta Velazquez, left and right but known as Lieutenant Harry T. Buford. Women posing as men was more common in the Civil War than most realize.

interview with The Railsplitter "did not influence me in the least with regard to my opinions concerning the rights or wrongs of the contest between the North and the South."

Hearing the Federals planned an all out fight in Kentucky, she knew that Confederate General Leonidas Polk had occupied Columbus, Kentucky on September 4, 1861, in direct violation of Kentucky's neutrality, a move that precipitated General U.S. Grant's moving to Paducah shortly thereafter. So dressed again as Lieutenant Harry T. Buford, she headed for Columbus, Kentucky.

"The Vicksburg Campaign Trail" says that at a time as many as 19,000 Confederate troops were stationed at Columbus near where the Ohio meets the Mississippi River. Over 140 heavy artillery and a gigantic chain with links weighing twenty pounds, later called "Pillow's Folly" for Confederate General Gideon Pillow, who had occupied nearby Hickman, Kentucky, was stretched across the river to the Missouri side, along with mines and floating gun boats, long lengths of trenches with an abatis, and two smaller forts outside of Columbus, so many emplacements that Columbus became known as the "Gibraltar of the West."

Harper's Weekly for March 29, 1862 describes in detail all the equipment and guns abandoned after the Confederates left Columbus, including the "celebrated one-hundred-and twenty pounder, Lady Polk," a rifled Dahlgren gun that wounded Polk when it exploded on

November 11, 1861. So many guns, so much equipment, so many men underline the aptness of the nickname given to this massive military installation.

A veteran of two battles now, Velazquez admits that her attitude toward soldiers had changed considerably: "My experiences—I do not allude to the mere hardships of a soldier's life—had not all been of the most pleasurable kind. I had learned much concerning some of the very weak points of human nature; that all men are not heroes who wished to be considered as such; that self-seeking was more common than patriotism; that mere courage sufficient to face the enemy in battle is not a very rare quality, and is frequently associated with meanness of spirit; that it is easier to meet the enemy bravely in battle, than it is to exercise one's brains so as to meet him most effectively; that great names are not always worthily borne by great men, and that a spirit of petty jealousy is even more prevalent in a camp than it is in a girl's boarding school." So when she arrived and reported to General Leonidas Polk in Columbus, asking for duty, she was a different soldier.

She observed that Columbus "was one of the liveliest places I had ever visited, or a least it seemed so that evening. There was an immense amount of bustle and confusion, and everything seemed to indicate that the campaign in this region was being pushed with considerable energy." Not aware that he was addressing a woman, when General Leonidas Polk assigned duty he said he wanted to use Lieutenant Buford in the detective corps. Elated at first because of earlier undercover experience, Buford soon learned that to Polk "detective duty" meant "to run on the trains and examine passes, furlough, and leaves of absence; and ...place anyone under arrest who was not traveling with the right kind of papers, or who was unprovided with papers of any kind."

As it happened, the lieutenant would soon be tested when General Lucius Polk, Leonidas' nephew, boarded the train without proper papers.

"Have you a pass?" Lieutenant Buford asked the general.

"No," said he. "Won't you let me go through without one?"

"No, sir, I cannot pass anyone. My orders are very strict, especially with regards to officers and soldiers," Buford replied.

"Well," the general said, "don't you could go back on your orders for once? Did you never favor a friend in this line?" Polk asked.

"Sir, I know no friends in connection to my duty, or general orders," the young officer insisted.

"Well, what are you going to do in my case, for I haven't got any pass," the general announced.

"I will send you back to headquarters, under guard," Buford retorted.

"But do you know, sir, that I am General Polk?" the general replied with a sense of insolence in his voice.

"I don't care, sir, who you are; you can't travel on this line without a pass, even if you are Jeff Davis himself," Buford thundered.

At that point, Polk announced that he did indeed have a pass and told Buford that he was just testing him. By this time, Buford said that "I was very badly vexed, however, that he should have attempted to play such a trick upon me, and have doubted my honor." In fact, Buford was so upset that when he returned to General Leonidas Polk and told the story, Buford promptly resigned, and left Polk's command.

Initially deciding to go back to Virginia, Buford heard that there would be heavy fighting in other parts of Kentucky, and so headed for Bowling Green, accompanied by a Colonel Bacon and a Captain Billingsley, hoping to report to General William Joseph Hardee, known as "Reliable" Hardee. Somehow detouring, Buford ended up fighting in the Battle of Rowletts Station, also known as the Battle of Woodsonville, or the Battle of Green River, near Munfordville, Kentucky, which occurred on December 17, 1861.

According to "The Battle of the Bridge" organization, under orders from Union General Don Carlos Buell, General Alexander McD. McCook went to Nolin, while Confederates placed themselves in a defensive position on the Green River close to Munfordville. On December 10th, McCook moved toward enemy lines, while the Confederates destroyed part of the Louisville and Nashville Railroad bridge. The Yankees then began building a pontoon bridge across the river. By December 17th, the bridge was complete and the Boys in Blue crossed the river and met enemy troops just below Woodsonville. Fighting broke out between the eight Union companies and a bigger phalanx of Rebels. Aware that the Rebels might want to outflank them, Union Colonel August Willich withdrew, as did the Rebels, too. Estimated casualties from the engagement numbered 40 Union and 91 Confederate soldiers, including Colonel Benjamin Terry, leader of Terry's Texas Rangers.

Of the fight, Velazquez says that she "took part in the fight at Woodsonville, on Green River, and faced the enemy as valiantly as anybody," punctuating her case as equal to the task in spite of being in reality a woman.

It should be noted, too, that in her autobiography she does correctly name Colonel Terry as one of the casualties, adding evidence to her veracity as a soldier truly present at the battle.

She said that "the affair at Woodsonville was something of a diversion from the monotony of camp life, but it did not satisfy my ambition or my intense desire for active service; and coming to the conclusion that lounging around Bowling Green and vicinity was much too slim a business for me, I decided to shift my quarters to where there was a somewhat better prospect of hard fighting to be done."

As Lieutenant Buford, she fought at Fort Donelson and Shiloh, lost two more husbands and eventually married for the fourth time, worked as a spy after being discovered to be a woman when she was wounded, and traveled to the Midwest, England, Canada, and France on missions of intrigue in one form or another.

After the war, she spent time in Venezuela, traveled to Utah, Colorado, New Mexico, Texas, and California, before dying in Austin, Nevada in 1897.

Her time in Kentucky as Lieutenant Harry T. Buford was short, but it is significant that, like many other places, she was not discovered to be the woman she was. To quote Sylvia Hoffert again, as Lieutenant Harry T. Buford and Loreta Velazquez and the many other aliases she used in her time, she had an "astonishing ability to travel North as well as South with little or no difficulty, using charm and guile as her most effective passport."

Blood and Smoke:
Kentuckian Major Walker Taylor's Plot to Abduct President Lincoln

Every couple of years, commercial and university presses roll out yet another book on President Abraham Lincoln's assassination. In excess of thirty and climbing, these works have approached the murder of The Great Emancipator from odd and interesting angles: some concentrate on just the assassin John Wilkes Booth, while others look for larger conspiracy theories that often far exceed the evidence.

While Presidents Garfield and McKinley also fell from an assassin's bullet, only the assassination of President John F. Kennedy on November 22, 1963, approaches the intense and abiding interest in the circumstances surrounding the death of Lincoln.

Each generation of scholars re-tells the story of what happened to Lincoln on April 14, 1865, and each generation sees the subject of the assassination as a unquenchable thirst Americans can never have slaked. Americans and even Europeans buy books that seem to promise a new view of the events at Ford's Theatre in a new light. But readers, in large part, are disappointed when they meet the same cast of characters dressed in new gowns, but still the same old characters performing in the same old tragedy.

Immediately after Lincoln's murder, the North quickly concluded that Booth and the principals were in league with the Confederacy in some sinister plot to turn the Civil War in their favor. After all, wouldn't having Lincoln out of the way spark the dying embers of the Confederate States of America? Doesn't the fact that other members of Lincoln's cabinet were also targets for assassination indicate that the Confederacy was involved at the highest levels? Yet despite extensive investigations shortly after the assassination and in the last 143 years, no convincing evidence has made the case that the Rebel government had anything to do with Lincoln's assassination, the suspicions lingered then and do now.

But what most Americans don't know is that there was a Confederate plot considered at the highest level to remove Lincoln from his presidency, a plot, indeed, that involved the nephew of a former President of the United States and a Kentuckian.

His name was Major Walker Taylor, born near Louisville on February 17, 1826, the son of Hancock Taylor, the brother of President Zachary Taylor, a popular Mexican War hero. Fortunately, J.B. Nation, a former Kentuckian from Daviess County, recently gathered important information about Major Taylor. Nation notes that shortly after the War between the States broke out, Major Taylor joined the Rebel army, first serving under another Kentuckian, General Simon Bolivar Buckner, and somehow escaping when Buckner was forced to surrender at Fort Donelson, but suffering from a nasty wound to the throat and cheek.

According to an article in *Confederate Veteran* magazine and other sources, after secretly recovering back in Louisville, Taylor somehow managed to convince another uncle, Union General Joseph Pannell Taylor, to let the younger Taylor stay with him on a visit to Washington, D.C. While there, Major Taylor, who had a flair for intrigue anyway, managed to attend a public reception at the White House, where he met President Lincoln, the President unaware that Taylor was anything but a loyal Union soldier from Kentucky.

Striking up a conversation, Lincoln noticed Taylor's war wound and asked him where he received his battle scar.

Taylor responded, "At Fort Donelson."

Lincoln then went on to compliment Grant and his soldiers who had given the Union its first significant victory in the west.

After the reception, Taylor stayed around Washington a few more days, studying Lincoln's daily routine, all the while plotting just how and when he would abduct the President, planning the details carefully to insure success when the time would come.

Then Taylor slipped past the Union lines and hastily set out for Richmond to speak personally with Confederate President Jefferson Davis. Major Taylor knew that Davis would see him, since Davis' first wife, Sarah Knox Taylor, who had died early in their marriage, was in fact Taylor's cousin, somebody Davis had known for sometime.

Kentuckian Walker Taylor: nephew of President Taylor, proposed a daring scheme to C.S.A. President Jefferson Davis.

Taylor probably thought Davis would jump at the chance to capture Lincoln, but he was to be disappointed.

A witness to the conversation, Colonel William Preston Johnson, Davis' aide-de-camp, said that Taylor began by telling the Confederate president, "Mr. Davis, I want to bring Lincoln a prisoner to you in this city."

"O, pshaw," Davis remarked in surprise, "How can such a thing as that be done?"

Taylor answered him, "Just as easily as walking out of this town." Taylor continued, "I came across the Potomac at no great distance from Washington, and while I was there I watched Lincoln's habits closely and know his outgoing and incoming. I tell you, sir, that I can bring him across that river just as easily as I can walk to your doorstep."

Davis seemed interested.

"How could you do it?"

"Lincoln," Taylor told him, "does not leave the White House until evening, or near twilight, and then with only a driver, he takes a lonely ride two or three miles in the country to a place called the Soldier's Home, which is his summer residence."

Taylor had done his homework and he detailed to Davis just how Lincoln's capture would take place.

"My point is to collect several of these Kentuckians whom I see about here doing nothing and who are brave enough for such a thing as that, and capture Lincoln, run down the Potomac, and cross him over just where I crossed, and the next day you will have him."

Davis, though, shook his head. "I cannot give my authority, Walker. In the first place, I suppose Lincoln is a man of courage. He has been in Indian wars and is a Western man. He would undoubtedly resist being captured. In that case, you would kill him. I could not stand the imputation of having consented to let Mr. Lincoln be assassinated."

Then, Davis began to consider the political implications of Taylor's scheme. "Our cause could not stand it. Besides, what value would he be to us as a prisoner? Lincoln is not the government of the Federal power. He is merely the political instrument there." Davis went on, "If he were brought to Richmond, what would we do with him? He would have to be treated like a magistrate of the North, and we have neither the time nor the provision."

He concluded: "No, sir, I will not give my authority to abduct Lincoln."

The writer in *Confederate Veteran* notes that Taylor never thought about the possibility of assassinating Lincoln. "The iron-willed Kentuckian simply desired to capture the Chief Executive of the United States and to retain him as a prisoner of war. …Was this refusal to sanction the proposed abduction mere sentiment? No, but it was manhood and wisdom. Thus it is seen that Davis not only did not desire the assassination of Lincoln, but refused to countenance even a possibility of it."

Several historians have commented on Taylor's plot to capture Lincoln. William A. Tidwell's *Retribution* says that Taylor's proposed intrigue was just one of many plots to either capture or assassinate Lincoln and places Taylor's plot within that broad context. William Hanchett's *The Lincoln Murder Conspiracies* also mentions the Taylor plan, and, like Tidwell, records Taylor's as one of many others designed to crop the head of the Union government.

But what about President Davis himself, somebody especially sensitive to rumors after Lincoln's assassination that had the Confederate leader intimately involved in Lincoln's assassination? Did Davis ever say any more about his meeting with Major Taylor?

More than twenty-four years after the war and after he had been released from prison, the former Confederate president wrote Major Taylor back in Louisville, just months before he died, asking Taylor to confirm what went on during their conversation in the early summer of 1862. Even two decades after Lincoln's assassination, Davis wanted to make sure his facts were straight.

His letter to Taylor, now kept in the Library of Virginia, began:

Beauvoir, Miss., August 31, 1889

My Dear Sir:

Your attention has, no doubt, been sometimes attracted to the revived, though baseless, accusation against me as having been connected with attempts to assassinate President Lincoln.

As you were the only man who ever talked to me on the subject of his capture, or at least the only one who I believed intended to do what he proposed, and that was carefully guarded against any design to kill, the purpose being to get the advantage of possession alive, I thought I would write to you for such recollection as you retain of your proposition to capture and my declining to entertain it on the ground that the attempt would probably involve the killing instead of bringing away the captive alive. It has been so long since I saw you that I may well ask how you are and how it fares with you.

I am, as ever, affectionately yours,

Jefferson Davis

As the letter indicates, Taylor's plot was real, and he did discuss it with Davis, and Davis would not approve the plan to abduct Lincoln. But the letter seems to have had another purpose: To put to rest the "baseless" rumors that he had anything at all to do with Lincoln's assassination, since, as he says, Taylor was "the only man who ever talked to me on the subject of his capture" and that Davis refused to be involved in any scheme that "would probably involve the killing" of Lincoln.

Given the lack of any real security to guard Lincoln, it is easy to speculate that Taylor, indeed, could have been successful at either abducting Lincoln or even murdering him.

In rejecting Taylor's plan, President Davis did show not only good political sense, but also the good moral sense that even in war, some measures are still out of the bounds of decency.

John Wilkes Booth, however, obviously disagreed.

Kentucky's Corporal Andrew Jackson Smith: Civil War Hero for his Country and for African Americans

On March 2, 1863, Frederick Douglass, the former slave turned abolitionist and spokesperson for African Americans both before and after the Civil War, stood tall and straight. In a thunderous voice, he called his black brothers to arms: "Action! Action! not criticism, is the plain duty of this hour!"

His booming voice spoke in haste: "There is no time for delay. The time is at the flood that leads to fortune." "Liberty," he emphasized, "won by white men would lack half its luster. Who would be free themselves must strike the first blow."

And then he reduced his call to a saying all would understand: "Better even to die free than to live slaves! This is the sentiment of every brave colored man among us."

Douglass acutely realized that African American soldiers had an important stake in the internecine war. They, of course, were aware that a Union victory not only meant freedom for them and their families, but also it represented a real opportunity for them to gain respect from white people, to "prove themselves," in other words.

For some, it is difficult to imagine a time when any person of any race would have to "prove" their worth, but it was very simply that way in nineteenth century America, where the stereotypes ran from the innate intellectual inferiority of the African race, to the commonly held belief "that the Negro shrinks from peril and that at best he may follow blindly where others, the white soldiers, lead," as one white leader phrased it.

Douglass, however, believed that "once the black man gets upon his person the brass letters, U.S., let him get an eagle on his button, and a musket on his shoulder and bullets in his pocket, and there is no power on earth which can deny that he has earned the right of citizenship in the United States."

But those prejudices against the black race predominated not only the South, where, according to census figures, 3,953,760 were enslaved, but also in the newly settled Midwest, and in other parts of the fledgling country where the possibility of black emancipation threatened the jobs of many lower class laborers.

Indeed, in 1858, in his debates with Stephan Douglas for the senate seat from Illinois, even Abraham Lincoln avowed that he didn't believe in the social equality of the Negro. While, certainly, Lincoln believed in granting blacks certain rights, including emancipation, he did not see them as his intellectual equals. As historian John T. Hubbell points out, "the laws of Kentucky, Indiana, Illinois–in common with those of other political jurisdiction within the United States–held the African to be less than a citizen, less than a person."

So shortly after the war began, early in his administration, when Lincoln began receiving subtle pressure from within his administration to use African Americans as soldiers, he quickly balked at the idea. He was willing to turn his head to allow freed slaves to serve the military in building bridges, repairing roads, and other menial tasks, but he was careful not to openly endorse the idea of using African American soldiers in combat.

As Hubbell notes, Lincoln feared the reaction from the border states, especially Kentucky, to seeing blacks in blue Union uniforms, patrolling the hills and plains of the Bluegrass State. For Kentucky, at the outset of the war, was a deeply enslaved state with more slave owners than any other state except Georgia and Virginia, a total of 225,483 slaves and 38,645 slave owners. In fact, in 1860, nearly 20% of the population in Kentucky was enslaved, with only 4.5% of blacks in the state free.

So Kentuckians could argue that in spite of the large number of slaves, the state had voted, even under strong pressure, both within and outside of the state, to stay in the union, while their Southern neighbors chose to secede. Didn't Kentucky deserve to retain her slaves as a reward for her loyalty? They asked.

But Lincoln was anything but politically naive. As the war wore on, and more and more white men fell in the slaughter, he gradually realized that in spite of the draft, he still needed soldiers.

Quietly, even as early as September 25, 1861, blacks began to enlist first in the navy. By the middle of 1862, things began to change when Lincoln did not openly advocate the use of black soldiers, yet he subtly allowed members of his cabinet to put into place the mechanisms for enlisting African Americans. He supported his decision, in some part, using the language employed in The Emancipation Proclamation of January 1, 1863, as a justification.

Hubbell notes that next, the adjutant general of the army, Lorenzo Thomas, who won considerable praise from Lincoln, went to the Mississippi Valley to enlist as many black troops as possible and round up white officers and enlisted men who were willing to take commissions in these same black regiments.

In many ways, Lincoln's political instincts told him that rather than abruptly announce a radical change in policy regarding enlisting blacks, he chose to ease the country into accepting blacks in Union uniforms.

It certainly could be argued that Lincoln's policy worked in Kentucky, for by the end of the war the state had provided the Union with 23,703 African American soldiers, more, in fact, than any other state except Louisiana.

The enlistment of so many African American soldiers also had the effect of virtually destroying slavery in Kentucky when more and more black men, along with their families, left bondage to join up, flooding places like Camp Nelson in Jessamine County, one of the few places nationally where African American soldiers were trained. Later, by December 18, 1865, the Thirteenth Amendment had been ratified, freeing the 40,000 remaining slaves in the Bluegrass State.

Yet in many ways, Kentucky continued to show a stubborn side, refusing to emancipate its few remaining slaves until ratification of the Thirteenth Amendment, and even withholding Kentucky's ratification until March 18, 1976.

Most black units were enlisted not in state units, like the 22nd Kentucky Infantry, but in regiments like the 114th U.S. Colored Infantry. Massachusetts, plagued by a labor shortage in the textile mills and a depleted supply of men who had gone West, was an exception.

The Bay State began recruiting blacks beyond the state's borders, in Pennsylvania, and even into the Mississippi Valley and Union-occupied portions of the South, all to form state units of black men from a variety of regions of the United States.

According to Civil War scholar Richard Abbott, at the time of the war, Massachusetts only had a total of 1,973 blacks eligible to serve, so in order to meet enlistment quotas, she had to resort to other means and began recruiting outside the state.

After all, the editor of the *Boston Commonwealth*, snidely remarked, a "great law of political economy forbids a country to drain out its best industry into the wasteful channels of war."

Of course, the congressman from Kentucky, Aaron Harding, didn't care much for the idea of Massachusetts filling their draft quotas with Kentucky slaves: "Their effort is to throw the burden of their share of fighting in this war upon the Negroes they may procure from other states."

Soon, though, Massachusetts had their body of black soldiers. Of course, the most celebrated of those units was the Massachusetts 54th, the subject of the recent movie, "Glory." It was that unit who refused pay until each black soldier was given the same pay as white soldiers, and they soon proved their worth in battle.

But still another unit from Massachusetts composed largely of black soldiers had attracted the attention of a runaway slave from western Kentucky. His story in fact helps to symbolize not only the African Americans' struggle to be free, but also the uncommon bravery of the black soldiers of the day.

The records of Andrew Jackson Smith's early life are scant, with many based on family stories handed down through generations, since records on slaves were rarely kept. But late in life, Corporal Smith did sit for an interview with the newspaper *National Tribune* on March 21, 1929, to discuss his life.

Smith was born September 3, 1843, believed to be the son of his master, Elijah Smith, and a slave identified only as Susan. At ten years old, he was assigned the job of transporting customers across the Cumberland River, a job he performed for another eight years.

When the war broke out, his master quickly joined the Confederate forces by September of 1861 and was off to war. In January of 1862, Elijah Smith returned home ostensibly to retrieve Andrew and take him back to the Confederate lines to serve as the master's personal servant, something he had not told Andy about.

But another slave, Alfred Bissell, overheard a conversation between Elijah Smith and another man in which Andy's master revealed his intentions of taking Andy back with him, an onerous task Andy was not willing to do.

Corporal Andrew Jackson Smith: One of Kentucky's war heroes. Library of Congress photo.

Knowing about the war through his job, Smith and Bissell secretly set out for Smithland, Kentucky, some twenty-five miles away. Smith knew that companies B and I of the 41st Illinois were stationed there, and the two runaways hoped the Union soldiers, whose duty was to patrol the Cumberland and Ohio Rivers, would take them in.

So Smith and Bissell walked all night through a "constant rain" until a "sudden change in temperature" froze their shirtsleeves and stuck to their bodies. When the sun came up the next morning, the two runaways had made it to the 41st Illinois lines. The pickets took the two to the encampment where the half-frozen pair were fed and given warm clothes.

Smith soon became the manservant of Major John Warner of Clinton, Illinois, and quickly the 41st was on the move, first to support Union General U.S. Grant's victories at Forts Donelson and Henry, major triumphs for the Union forces in the west. Next, they were on to Shiloh, where, on April 6-7th, the 41st again fought in support of Grant and General William T. Sherman in one of the bloodiest days of fighting of the war.

In the fighting, Major Warner had two horses shot from underneath him, which Smith quickly replaced, even going so far as securing a Confederate mount when the major was in need of a third horse. All during the battle, Smith stayed close by, so close, indeed, that a minie ball hit him in the left ear, but fortunately rolled under the skin to the center of his forehead. The surgeon quickly removed the lead ball, but Smith was left with a scar for life.

For some reason, Major Warner, now Colonel Warner, as a result of his meritorious service, returned to Illinois in November, and took young Smith with him.

While in Clinton, during the early part of 1863, Smith heard about the formation of the 54th Massachusetts, either by hearing Colonel Warner read about it, or from Massachusetts' recruiters in the area, and Smith knew he wanted to join up.

As Smith tells it, he then contacted military authorities in Boston, asked for transportation money, and he, along with 55 other Illinois African Americans, arrived in Boston to join the 54th Massachusetts, one of the three places in the nation besides New Orleans and Camp Nelson, Kentucky where blacks could enlist and be trained.

According to the regiment's historian, Bennie J. McRae, the unit, the 55th Massachusetts, began to form in May of 1863 in Readville, Massachusetts. Smith says he arrived on May 16th and quickly became a part of Company B. On June 22nd, the last of the recruits had arrived for training, and by July 21st, according to other records, the regiment was on its way to Newberne, North Carolina to be a part of the African Brigade, Vogde's Division, 10th Corps.

For a couple of months, the regiment dug entrenchments and performed other non-combat duties at Folly Island, South Carolina, but eventually they fought a bloody battle at Honey Hill on November 30, 1864, where Smith would achieve his glory.

The battle itself was a clash between Union and Confederate forces as a part of Sherman's March to the Sea. Union forces, split off from the main body of Sherman's army, attempted to secure the Charleston and Savannah Railroad. If the Boys in Blue had wrestled control of it, the other Union forces of Sherman would have a straight shot to Savannah, and, perhaps, bring an earlier end to the war.

But the Confederates were dug in on a road to Grahamville, South Carolina, bordered by a swamp on one side, and a dense forest on the other. To add to the Union's woes, the road itself was also heavily fortified behind a massive impregnable earthworks.

So the only way forward, unfortunately, was the road, if the Union forces under General John P. Hatch had any chance of routing the stubborn Rebels.

Faced with no other options, the Union forces charged the Confederates several times. Smith said he was a part of three charges himself that resulted in losing a third of their men.

Smith was then a part of the color guard, usually an assembly of about twelve men, whose responsibility it was to protect the battle flags of that particular unit at all costs. To allow the battle flag to fall on the ground during battle was to besmirch the bravery of those who looked to their flag as a symbol of unity and valor and honor.

Indeed, the color guard was to hold the flag high throughout the course of battle, no matter how dangerous it might be. So if the flag bearer was wounded or killed, one other member of the color guard rushed forward to catch the flag before it touched the ground. Similarly, to allow the enemy to capture a unit's flag was, besides defeat, the ultimate military insult.

What Corporal Andrew Jackson Smith of the 55th Massachusetts, from Lyon County, Kentucky, did next is recorded in his government citation.

The document reads, in part, that Smith and his comrades were "forced into a narrow gorge crossing a swamp in the face of the enemy's position, the 55th Color Sergeant was killed by an exploding shell, and Corporal Smith took the Regimental Colors from his hand and carried them through heavy grape and canister fire. Although half of the officers and a third of the enlisted men engaged in the fight were killed or wounded, Corporal Smith continued to expose himself to enemy fire by carrying the colors throughout the battle.

"Through his actions, the Regimental Colors of the 55th Infantry regiment were not lost to the enemy. Corporal Andrew Jackson Smith's extraordinary valor in the face of deadly enemy fire is in keeping with the highest traditions of military service and reflect great credit upon him, the 55th Regiment, and the United States Army."

Unfortunately for Corporal Smith, his Congressional Medal of Honor was not awarded to him in his lifetime. President William Jefferson Clinton, 137 years after the event that brought him such honor, presented the medal to several of Smith's descendants on January 16, 2001.

Dr. Burt G. Wilder, the regimental surgeon of the 55th, waged a lifelong battle to get Smith the recognition he deserved, but in the confusion of battle that day at Honey Hill, nobody was able to document Smith's bravery.

Yet Smith's descendants wouldn't give up, and mounted a vigorous campaign, guided in part by a professor at Illinois State University, who contacted a congressman, who, in turn, finally got the military to recognize Smith's uncommon bravery at Honey Hill.

At the ceremony, Army Chief of Staff, General Eric K. Shinseki, noted ironically that "Corporal Smith was a man who fought for freedoms he did not fully enjoy himself. He was a man who fought for a concept of democracy that had not yet fully recognized his own inalienable rights. And he was a man who fought both an enemy on the battlefield and a prejudice within his own Army."

Corporal Smith, who was later promoted to Color Sergeant, survived the war, mustered out of the service on August 29, 1865, and went back to Clinton, Illinois for a time. But by 1866, he returned to Eddyville in Lyon County to spend the remainder of his life there, using his mustering out pay to purchase some land and be near his mother and three sisters.

He said that he also visited with his "old playmates, who were ex-Confederate soldiers. I then saw my former owner, who came to me and gave me good advice. He told me that he was as poor as I," Smith concluded.

Smith lived a long life, passing away on March 4, 1932 at 89 years old. He lies buried in Mount Pleasant Cemetery in Grand Rivers, Kentucky, in Livingston County, near Smithland, with a fitting headstone inscribed with a grand design designating him as a Medal of Honor winner.

While Smith hardly received the respect and recognition he deserved in his lifetime, he must have felt confident that his life had a real purpose, fighting for his emancipation and the emancipation of millions of African Americans, and knowing, above all, that he had truly done his part.

Greensburg's General Edward Hobson: An Ordinary Soldier Doing Extraordinary Things

In Civil War circles, Union General Edward Hobson of Greensburg is known for two things: capturing fellow Kentuckian, Confederate General John Hunt Morgan, and then later being captured by General John Hunt Morgan, creating a military protocol nightmare.

While much of what we know about him comes from limited sources, including the scholarship of Albert Nutgrass, General Edward Hobson's story starts in Green County, Kentucky, where he was born on July 11, 1825, one of eight children to William Hobson, born in January 1788, and Lucy Kirtley Hobson, born November 8, 1793, who married on March 14, 1814. Both parents had crossed the mountains in search of new and more rewarding opportunities in the early life of Kentucky. Edward's father, a veteran of the War of 1812, opened a hardware store in Greensburg in 1808, and by the time Edward was of age, William Hobson had a successful business, which also included the Branch Bank of Kentucky in Greensburg.

Edward received a spotty education and enrolled at Centre College, but his health failed, and he disliked school so much that he dropped out, wandering the South as a hog drover until finally saving enough money by 1846 to open his own dry goods store in Greensburg.

But by this time, war with Mexico was in the air, and much of Kentucky, despite some dissent, was caught up in military fever, including the young Edward Hobson. He quickly became a part of a group of ardent soldiers called the "Green River Boys," particularly Company A of the Second Kentucky Infantry. Nutgrass quotes an article in the *Baltimore Patriot*, which trumpeted that "there existed something in the very air of Kentucky that made a soldier," and young Edward Hobson was one of them. Hobson was elected a second lieutenant in a unit led by the son of the powerful United States senator from Kentucky, Henry Clay, named Colonel Henry Clay, Jr., who was later killed in the war leading a charge at the Battle of Buena Vista on February 23, 1847.

Hobson saw limited action in the war, but managed to earn the rank of first lieutenant by the war's end for his service at the Battle of Buena Vista; but with the war over and victory assured, Hobson returned to Greensburg to pursue the mercantile and banking business with renewed vigor. On October 12, 1847, he married Kate Adair, the niece of Governor John Adair of Mercer County, who served from 1820-1824. The marriage eventually produced six children.

With the fall of Fort Sumter on April 14, 1861, war was again imminent in Kentucky. By autumn, Hobson realized that General Simon Bolivar Buckner intended to use the State Guard in support of the Confederacy, so Hobson, along with five companions, reasoning that the money in the Greensburg bank was not safe, carried $140,000 in gold, silver, and currency from the Greensburg bank to the Bank of Kentucky in Louisville, the only branch bank south of Louisville to do so.

Although a slave owner, Hobson realized that the preservation of the Union was of utmost importance and soon sided with the Federal government. Simon Cameron, Lincoln's Secretary of War, appointed Hobson as Colonel of the Thirteenth Kentucky Infantry (earlier known as the Second Kentucky Infantry), one of many assignments for the Greensburg native. Even though there are some discrepancies, Hobson probably formally mustered in on December 30, 1861 at Camp Hobson, near Greensburg, and assumed his colonelcy on January 1, 1862. While biographer Nutgrass admits there is some confusion about the chain of command, he concludes that Hobson's Thirteenth was eventually under General Thomas L. Crittenden, son of the famous Kentucky senator, author of the famous Crittenden Compromise. The Thirteenth, along with other units, made its way to Bowling Green, the early capital of the Confederacy in Kentucky.

But by April 6th, the Thirteenth found itself near a little church near Pittsburg Landing, known in the annals of war as Shiloh, ironically a Hebrew word that meant "place of peace."

Hobson and his men of the Thirteenth found themselves in the thick of it, a part of the Eleventh Brigade, under the command of General J.T. Boyle, along with the Nineteenth and Fifty-Ninth Ohio, and the Ninth Kentucky. One veteran of Shiloh described it as "a very bloody place," so the whole nation truly knew, after Shiloh, that war would be protracted and a murderous affair. Hobson himself, writing of his experiences at Shiloh wrote that "it was a terrible affair...dead men and horses covered the earth," but, in a stroke of immodestly, Hobson said that, "you will see in the reports shortly published that the General mentions me as behaving in good style." Hobson and his men then participated in the successful siege at Corinth, arriving by June in Chattanooga.

After a short leave of absence and a reorganization of forces in Kentucky, Hobson was next assigned to Munfordville on the Green River, an important assignment because the small Kentucky town was on a direct highway between Louisville and Nashville, and thus supply lines that headed south. His mission there, besides training troops, was to guard the railroad in the area, an assignment that led to his first confrontation with a man responsible for some of Hobson's most glorious moments and, at the same time, some of his most inglorious: The "Thunderbolt of the Confederacy," Lexington's own, cavalry leader, John Hunt Morgan.

Commonly called "The Christmas Raid," Morgan left Alexandria, Tennessee and crossed into Kentucky at Tompkinsville on December 23, 1862. From a Confederate prisoner, Hobson learned that Morgan was headed his way, so the Union general sent troops out to intercept the charismatic Confederate leader, finally clashing with a portion of Morgan's men near Cave City at Bear Wallow on Christmas Day. After some sporadic skirmishing in the area around Bacon Creek and Munfordville late that night, by morning, Morgan and his men had gone, headed north through Upton, Elizabethtown, and looping back at Lebanon Junction, Bardstown, Springfield, Lebanon, toward Campbellsville, meeting significant resistance at Tebbs Bend before escaping back into Tennessee to Smithville. For his efforts at Munfordville, Hobson received credit, although really little action ensued there. On April 29, 1863, Hobson was promoted to brigadier general, a long sought after commission that pleased Hobson and his fellow Green Countians. Nutgrass notes that Hobson, "deserved the new rank probably as much as any comparable officer in the service. He lived up to the honor as well as most other volunteer officers."

But his next encounter with the elusive Morgan was considerably more satisfying for Hobson, in spite of chasing Morgan across three states.

After another re-organization, Hobson and his men were commanded by General Henry M. Judah under what was now called the Third Division, all anticipating still another raid by Morgan and his men. Moving from Munfordville to Columbia to Carthage, Tennessee and then Tompkinsville, and next to Burkesville, Hobson, under Judah's command, frantically anticipated just where and when Morgan would re-appear. Judah finally assigned Hobson and his Second Brigade to guard the tiny community of Marrowbone, slightly northwest of the Cumberland River, near Burkesville.

General Edward Hobson, a Union citizen-soldier who chased General John Hunt Morgan over three states. Courtesy of the Kentucky Historical Society.

Finally, the long anticipated Morgan and some 2500 men started north from Sparta, Tennessee, and on July 2, 1863, crossed the Cumberland and headed north on what is commonly called Morgan's "Great Raid," Morgan met Hobson at his camp outside of Marrowbone in a skirmish that ironically allowed Morgan to collect his various scattered factions before resuming his push north, fooling Judah and allowing the wary "Thunderbolt of the Confederacy" an escape route.

Under orders now from General Ambrose Burnside, received on July 6th, in Lebanon, Hobson, along with General James Shackleford and Colonel Frank Lane Wolford, was to give chase after Morgan, with Hobson leading the mission. At Tebbs Bend, south of Campbellsville, Morgan lost seventy-one men in an ill-advised move. Morgan, then, lost his brother, Tom, in action in Lebanon, prompting Morgan to burn the city in revenge. Continuing north, Morgan raced through Springfield and Bardstown with Hobson close behind. Hobson sent a frantic telegraph to headquarters in Louisville, saying that "I am here for rations; cannot find any. My men are considerably exhausted but in fine spirits." By this time, Hobson deduced that Morgan was headed for either Elizabethtown or Brandenburg, and later that evening he wired Boyle that Morgan appeared bound for Brandenburg and requested a gunboat to be sent to the Ohio River community.

Meanwhile, Morgan had sent an advanced party ahead of him to secure boats to ferry Morgan and his men across the river into southern Indiana. In the early morning of July 8th, they were successful in finding both the *John T. McCombs* and the newly arrived *Alice Dean*, their means to invade what they called "Yankeeland." Morgan and the bulk of his men arrived in Brandenburg shortly after nine that foggy morning and quickly set about the business of getting troops and horses across the Ohio.

At the same time, Hobson and his men made it to Garnettsville, several miles east of Brandenburg on the eighth also, but didn't press on to Brandenburg, choosing instead to make camp, a move that his detractors describe as indicating that Hobson had a bad case of the "Morgan jitters." Hobson, however, said in his report to his superiors, that "we have pursued with all haste; have lost no time."

But the next day, Burnside didn't seem to think so, wiring General J.T. Boyle in Louisville and telling him that "Hobson should be ordered to follow close on Morgan. Can't you dispatch a boat or a messenger to him at once, with orders not to lose a moment's time? I am afraid he is too late as it is. He will be fully twenty-four hours behind Morgan, and I don't think his pursuit has been rapid. He ought to have been onto Morgan before his whole force crossed at Brandenburg."

In Hobson's defense, however, he showed no signs later or before in his persistent pursuit of Morgan to indicate that he feared Morgan enough to avoid engagement with the fellow Kentuckian.

The gunboat requested by Hobson, *The Springfield*, commanded by Ensign James Watson, filed a report on the same day, reporting that he had been engaging Morgan all day, and that Morgan had 10,000 men, several pieces of heavy artillery, and had batteries three places and was in control of the river. The figure of 10,000, of course, was five times the number of men Morgan actually had, but it indicates the kind of misinformation that panicked all of southern Indiana as Morgan made his way north toward Corydon, Indiana.

By early in the morning of the tenth, Hobson and his men had crossed the Ohio and were, in the words of General Boyle, in "hot pursuit." By July 11th, Hobson was in Salem, and there, and all along the way, Nutgrass records, Hobson was inundated by expressions of good will by local citizens who eagerly supplied the tired and hungry Union soldiers with eats like fried chicken. Hobson and those following him were seen as heroes pursuing that bandit Morgan, who, by now, had left Indiana and turned east into southern Ohio.

By this time, Judah and his men had resumed the chase. Morgan appeared to be headed for Meigs County, Ohio, particularly Buffington Island and the ford there. A battle that ensued there was led by Shackleford and his men and resulted in the capture of 750 of Morgan's now depleted men, including Morgan's second in command, Colonel Basil Duke.

But General Morgan escaped. To add insult to injury, General Judah suddenly appeared and took over the entire command, a move that Hobson rightly objected to. When informed, Burnside first seemed to waffle on who really was in command, but finally agreed that the mission should be Hobson's. Nutgrass blames Burnside for all the confusion about who was in command, arguing that Burnside did not "make clear his mind, and left the generals to decide."

By July 26th, near New Lisbon, Ohio, Shackleford, Wolford, and others captured what was left of Morgan and his ragtag men, who, along with Morgan, were summarily sent to the state prison in Columbus, treated not as prisoners of war, but as common outlaws. It was the end of an over 1000 mile chase and represented the deepest penetration of the Confederacy, proving, though in a limited sense, that the Rebels could bring the War between the States into Yankee territory, too.

As commander of the forces dogging Morgan, Hobson ultimately received credit for Morgan's capture and was generally regarded as a genuine war hero. As Nutgrass reports, Hobson was suitably feted for his deeds on the evening of July 27, 1863, in the Galt House in Louisville, and later treated similarly in his home town of Greensburg.

Unfortunately, this wasn't the end of Morgan and Hobson's contact with the swashbuckling general in gray with the handsome goatee and cavalier stature. Only this time, Hobson wouldn't be the man of the hour.

It was Morgan's turn.

After the capture of Morgan, Hobson went home for a short time to rest and recover from the over 1,000 mile chase. But he didn't stay long, and was quickly re-assigned back to Munfordville, where his primary duty was to guard south central Kentucky from the continuing problem of guerrillas. Much like General William Tecumseh Sherman, who had had his fill of guerrillas while stationed in Kentucky, and General Stephen Gano Burbridge, who as of June 1864, was in command of the District of Kentucky, Hobson had little sympathy for guerrillas.

But ordinary Kentucky citizens were quite confused by the actions of soldiers in both blue and gray. While Union soldiers would use valuable fence rails for campfires, the Rebels would "press," that is, confiscate, needed horses. In many cases, it just wasn't clear who the enemy was. As a result, Hobson spent much of his time trying to satisfy the victims of military action on both sides. This was the era of such infamous guerrillas as Champ Ferguson, Tinker Dave Beatty and "Sue Mundy," a time when Kentucky seemed to spell havoc, a time when the ordinary citizen, like it or not, was a daily participant in the war itself, a time when even simple county elections were fraught with a military flavor. Amid the chaos that was Kentucky, Washington seemed little concerned, its attention more on a victory that now seemed possible in more crucial places than the Commonwealth. "Kentuckians can take care of Kentucky" seemed to be the motto of those running the government.

Things got particularly bad in the mountains of eastern Kentucky and western Kentucky. In western Kentucky, Confederate General Adam "Stovepipe" Johnson went on a tear, burning courthouses all over the far western part of the state, convinced that these county seats were being used as Union recruiting stations. He, of course, had to be attended to, and Hobson did just that. But first, in the mountains, Hobson commanded the 13th Kentucky Cavalry and other Kentucky units and rode with Burbridge to Saltville, Virginia to destroy the vital salt works there on October 2, 1864. But the mission failed, and resulted in the massacre of black Union troops from the Fifth United States Colored Cavalry.

Yet of more concern was the fact that General John Hunt Morgan had escaped after four months in the Ohio prison and seemed bent on still another raid into Kentucky. Needless to say, the Federals were quite concerned, so under Burbridge's orders, Hobson left the mountains in a hurry and went on ahead towards central Kentucky. After considerable jockeying from place to place, Hobson and Morgan met again on June 1, 1864, just north of Cynthiana, Kentucky, at a place called Kellar's Bridge.

Caught in a crook in the Licking River, Hobson had little choice after intense fighting but to surrender, along with about 1300 other Union soldiers and Home Guards.

As Nutgrass explains it, the usual military protocol would be for Morgan to parole his prisoners and be on his way. Hobson and his soldiers would pledge not to fight until they had been exchanged for Confederate soldiers of equal rank in the same status.

But Hobson knew something that Morgan didn't, and that was that Burbridge was not far behind.

If Hobson could stall long enough, he reasoned, maybe Burbridge would arrive, relieve Hobson from the embarrassment of being captured, and clinch the victory for the Union forces.

So Hobson refused Morgan's first offer.

Morgan next offered Hobson terms in which Hobson would agree not to take up arms against the Rebels and not reveal information about Morgan and his troops.

Still stalling for time, Hobson refused the second offer.

Morgan offered Hobson a third option. Hobson would agree to try to effect an exchange, but if Hobson were not successful, he was to ride to Morgan's headquarters in Virginia and surrender.

With Burbridge not in sight and Morgan running out of patience, Hobson agreed to this third set of terms.

Several of Morgan's men then accompanied Hobson and his men to Falmouth to begin the process he agreed to. All bedded down for the night, they awakened in the morning confronting the problem of a Union provost marshal who had arrested everybody and declared that Hobson was still a prisoner and that the military brass would have to figure out what to do with him.

In other words, Hobson was a prisoner of Confederates who were also prisoners of the Union soldiers.

Hobson was in an awkward position, and it was quite an imbroglio.

Meanwhile, early on June 12th, Burbridge and his 2,400 men finally did arrive in Cynthiana, where Morgan had camped for the night instead of moving on. Although Morgan was not captured, the Rebs fled and many were taken prisoner in an early morning rout.

But what to do with Hobson and his men.

On June 21st, General-in-Chief Henry Halleck in Washington wrote to Burbridge saying, "If General Hobson and staff entered into any agreement or gave paroles not in accordance with the cartel they must be arrested, and the facts reported to the War department for its actions. It was their duty to compel the enemy to guard them, so as to prevent an escape or re-capture, and not to relieve him of that difficulty by any agreement. All paroled soldiers will be returned to the ranks and paroled officers reported for disobedience of orders."

Technically, Halleck was correct: Hobson had entered into an agreement not sanctioned by the cartel. As a result, Hobson was arrested, although obviously he protested. But fortunately for Hobson, Burbridge sent a message in which he argued that Hobson should "be relieved from arrest and be permitted to go on to duty." Hobson, too, argued his case at great length and detail. And, eventually, Hobson's superiors agreed, and he returned to duty.

Later, General John Hunt Morgan heard that Hobson had resumed duties, and on July 17th fired off a protest, saying "I cannot think there has been so flagrant a violation of faith as is herein indicated," and asked Burbridge "what has been the action of your Government in the premises?"

Of course, Morgan got no answer.

Hobson, quite tired of war and government by now, spent the remainder of the war chasing guerrillas and lodging complaints about the lack of equipment and supplies to a Federal government occupied with the long anticipated surrender in the East.

After the war, Hobson remained active: President Ulysses S. Grant appointed him a collector for the Internal Revenue, he served as a commander for the Grand Army of the Republic, he helped promote railroad construction in his native Green County, and he remained active in business. He died in Cleveland, Ohio at a G.A.R. meeting on September 14, 1901.

Nutgrass, in his reflective and considered evaluation of the importance of Edward Hobson to the Civil War, notes that while Hobson was not a brilliant military tactician or a great organizer and motivator of men, he was a part of the vast majority of men who served in the Civil War who had not graduated from West Point or the Naval Academy, but whose blood mingled with that of the highly trained officers.

Without those citizen soldiers, the Union could not have achieved victory, or in Nutgrass' words, "The Civil War was fought by great armies of volunteer soldiers led by volunteer officers commanded by professionals. The volunteer officers were the link between the ranks and the commanding generals. They were the link between the soldiers and home, and between the citizens of their state and military authority."

So, too, was General Edward Hobson.

Confederate General Hylan Benton Lyon: Fighting Hard and Raising Cain

Few people's lives beg for biography more than Kentuckian Hylan B. Lyon: orphan, Indian fighter, Confederate general, farmer and politician.

Hylan Benton Lyon was born on February 22, 1836, in present-day Lyon County (the county is named in honor of his uncle, Chittenden Lyon) on a farm called "Riverview," some two miles above Eddyville on the Cumberland River. Lyon was orphaned at the age of eight after the deaths of his father, Matthew Lyon, Jr. in 1839, and his mother, Elizabeth Martin Lyon, a native of Vermont, in 1844.

Under the guardianship of Fred H. Skinner, young Lyon received an education at the local schools, then went on to Masonic University at LaGrange, Kentucky and Cumberland College at Princeton, Kentucky before being accepted at the age of 16 to the United States Military Academy at West Point. He graduated nineteenth in a class of forty-eight in 1856.

Breveted a second lieutenant in the U.S. Second Artillery, Lyon began his military career at Fort Myers, Florida, where he helped in the removal of the Seminole Indians to Indian Territory. From there, Lyon was ordered to Fort Yuma, California, one of the hottest and dustiest assignments in the Army at the time. Kentucky historian Clauscine R. Baker tells the amusing story of how hot it was at Fort Yuma. Supposedly, one soldier at the fort died and went to hell. The same soldier came back a few days later for his overcoat and blankets because it was so much cooler in hell than it was at Fort Yuma.

From Fort Yuma, Lyon was sent to Washington Territory where he was involved in two battles with the Indians. He also witnessed the treachery of his commanding officer, who lured the Indian Chief Qualshm and his wife into the fort under the pretense of friendship but after disarming himself to make clear his amicable intentions, Qualshm was seized by soldiers and prepared to hang. According to Baker, "when the Indian was made to understand that he was to be hanged, he laid on the ground and could not be forced to stand up, so six soldiers took him in their arms and carried him to a leaning tree, over a limb of which a rope was thrown." As Baker writes, "no more mournful sounds were ever uttered than those made by Qualshm in begging for his life. He cried, 'Stop, friend, stop, friend, don't kill me. I will give you a great deal of money, a great many horses if you will not kill me,'" but Qualshm was ultimately hanged.

Soon thereafter, Lyon was granted leave to return home to Kentucky. While there, the Civil War broke out, so Lyon resigned his commission in the United States Army on April 30, 1861, and volunteered his services to the Confederacy. He assumed the rank of first lieutenant of artillery, but soon was appointed captain of Cobb's Battery. By January 1862, he was promoted to lieutenant colonel of the Eighth Kentucky Infantry, leading that regiment in its defense of Fort Donelson in northern Tennessee on the Cumberland River, a vital link in the defense of the upper South, and Tennessee especially.

According to Civil War historian S.W. Sanders, writing in *America's Civil War* magazine, Lyon and his regiment were holed up in trenches in rifle pits, just outside the fort. They took six hours of Union artillery bombardment, losing two dead and ten wounded. The following day Union troops continued to take shots at the Confederates. So when the Blue Coats attacked, Lyon and his men fought back, meeting the enemy in a grove outside the fort.

Lyon wrote that his men "fought gallantly, assisting to whip and drive back the enemy, sustaining the loss of 17 killed, 46 officers and men wounded, and one man missing." Soon, however, the fort was overrun.

While Lyon and his men could have possibly escaped from the besieged fort, as General Nathan Bedford Forrest did, Lyon and his men felt honor bound to surrender to the enemy. As a result, Lyon was taken prisoner, first incarcerated at Fort Warren in Boston Harbor and later moved to Johnson's Island in Ohio. After seven months as a prisoner, on August 15, 1862, Lyon was exchanged and promptly promoted to colonel.

According to historian Terry Jones, Lyon quickly made his way back through the Confederate lines and assumed command again of the Eighth Kentucky, fighting at Coffeeville, Champion Hill, and Vicksburg, where he and his command escaped during the siege there, and later fought at Missionary Ridge.

Although he and his regiment had performed admirably, Lyon still hadn't found his niche. But that was soon to change when he linked up again with General Nathan Bedford Forrest, the famed cavalry leader. Forrest was a self-taught military genius whom Union General William Tecumseh Sherman called "the most remarkable man our civil war produced on either side." Union General U.S. Grant called Forrest "that devil Forrest," so frustrating were Forrest and his cavalry to the Union side. Lyon quickly caught on to Forrest's system and fit neatly into Forrest's strategy of battle.

Perhaps nowhere else did Lyon prove his value to Forrest more than at Brice Cross Roads, Mississippi on June 10, 1864, when Forrest was ordered to try to interrupt General Sherman's supply lines as Sherman rolled toward Atlanta and on his ultimate March to the Sea.

Lieutenant Colonel Joseph B. Mitchell in *Decisive Battles of the Civil War*, calls Forrest's actions there "one of the most outstanding examples of brilliant tactics in American military history."

Once again, Forrest and his men used the famous "envelope" tactic, where one group fiercely charged from the front, while other groups charged both flanks, and a fourth group charged the enemy's rear, resulting in Union mass confusion and hysteria.

Lyon's 800, meeting 1500 of the enemy, was part of that great onslaught from the right of the Confederate line. As Sanders observes, Lyon's Brigade met soldiers from the Third and Ninth Illinois Cavalry "in a dense thicket of oak trees almost half a mile north of the crossroads. Lyon boldly attacked the Federal force and pushed it back."

With nearly twice as many enemy soldiers ahead of him, Lyon needed a strategy to equalize the numbers. He chose to try to bewilder the enemy by a bold charge in their direction, meeting the enemy head on. As Sanders notes, the tactic "confused the Federals who believed that more Confederate troops were lurking in the thicket." Sanders records that Forrest later wrote that Lyon's efforts helped contribute to a "crowning success over vastly superior forces." Then Forrest singled out Lyon who "displayed great gallantry during the day."

Another cavalry man, Bennett Young, in *Confederate Wizards of the Saddle* wrote that to Lyons "belongs the credit of having opened the greatest of all cavalry battles, and to have done more than any one Confederate officer, other than Forrest, to win the crushing defeat of the Union forces on that historic field."

No doubt because of his efforts in large part at Brice Cross Roads, on June 14, 1864, Lyon received the rank of brigadier general. He later served under Forrest in other forays in Mississippi and Tennessee until he replaced General Adam "Stovepipe" Johnson as commander of the District of Western Kentucky on September 26, 1864, where Lyon served until March 1865.

General Hylan Benton Lyon: Burning courthouses used for Union recruitment was his specialty. Courtesy of the Kentucky Historical Society.

Sanders argues that the powers in Richmond realized that wrestling Kentucky from Union hands would "take a competent and experienced general with expert knowledge of the area to pry the region from Union control."

So Lyon chose his hometown of Eddyville, Kentucky to begin his actions to re-take Kentucky and recruit men from the man-short Confederacy. As Sanders describes it, Lyon and his men rode into town at five o'clock in the morning with only about 40 soldiers and attacked a small contingency of Union soldiers holed up in the courthouse with 28 men, eight officers from an African American regiment, and 27 black recruits. After a show of force, the Federals surrendered and were paroled.

But a group of Union soldiers had captured Lyon's wife. Lyon quickly exchanged nine Union officers for her safety.

Convinced of the necessity of squelching Union recruiting efforts in the Commonwealth and hoping to add good Kentucky boys to the Confederate rolls, in December of 1864 he began a mission to burn county courthouses being used as recruiting stations across western Kentucky and other parts of the state. Lyon thus sought to divert Union attention away from Confederate general and fellow Kentuckian John Bell Hood's campaign in Nashville.

The first to be torched was Christian County's courthouse in Hopkinsville on December 12th. While the building burned, the county records were saved, but Lyon did acquire some clothing and a few men.

Next was the Trigg County courthouse in Cadiz, the following day, where the Union defenders fled and Lyon's men burned the building to the ground, sparing a man ill with smallpox inside. Again, the county records were saved.

From Cadiz, Lyon and his men moved on December 15th to Princeton in Caldwell County, where Union troops had fled upon hearing that Lyon was on his way from Eddyville. Once again, Lyon set fire to the courthouse, and once again the county records were saved.

Next on the list was Madisonville, county seat of Hopkins County, where on December 17th Lyon and his troops set fire to the courthouse and conscripted men for the Confederate cause, who later, incidentally, did not live up to their Confederate allegiance.

Moving east, Lyon and his men set out for Hartford, the county seat of Ohio County, where they set fire to the courthouse on December 20th, paroled the prisoners, and refrained from burning the county records after Dr. Samuel O. Peyton pleaded for their safety.

According to Mary Joseph Jones' *The Civil War in Hardin County, Kentucky*, Lyon and his charges next appeared in the Elizabethtown area where Lyon's troops at Nolin Station attacked a train loaded with Union troops and captured them after "a spirited resistance." Lyon moved on to Elizabethtown where they seized a garrison of 45 Union troops. The next day Lyon forced local citizens to secure firewood to burn two railroad bridges, while Lyon and his men also burned a stockade and a load of lumber before retreating upon the arrival of Federal troops.

On Christmas day of 1864, Lyon and his troops set fire to the Taylor County courthouse in Campbellsville, where some records were saved, but desertions among Lyon's men left him with just 250 men.

The seventh courthouse was in Burkesville, when on January

3, 1865, Lyon and his troops burned the Cumberland County courthouse. While there Lyon and his men robbed several stores and captured horses, but left Kentucky for the rest of the war.

Sanders reports that "as Lyon rode through western Kentucky conscripting men, plundering stores and burning courthouses, no Federal troops seemed able to stop him. He and his men were doing whatever they pleased." To continue, "Union officers begged for more troops, but because there was a lack of manpower, only small units of Federal cavalry could pursue Lyon...."

But at Red Hill, Alabama, in mid-January 1865, some Pennsylvania Cavalry troops thought they had him.

Although there are at least two versions of the story, Lyon himself tells the tale this way.

He was awakened one night, sleeping at a private residence when he heard someone say, "Halt. Dismount. Surround the house!" Lyon at first thought that the commotion was the activity of his own men.

Suddenly, however, someone knocked. Lyon said he got up and answered the door.

"Where is General Lyon?" the intruder asked.

"I am General Lyon. Who are you?" Lyon answered.

"I am Lieutenant Lyon of the Fifteenth Pennsylvania Cavalry. You are my prisoner."

General Lyon then asked that he be allowed to put on some clothes, and the Yankee officer consented, following Lyon into the room where the general's clothes were. In Lyon's words: "He very foolishly did not ask me for my arms but was so much rejoiced at capturing a General, believing that thereby his reputation was made that he forgot the small details necessary to hold a General after he is captured."

With fifty Union men surrounding the house, though, General Hylan B. Lyon's fate seemed to be sealed.

While he was dressing, someone outside shouted, "Here comes the cavalry! Here comes the cavalry!"

Thinking that General Lyon's men had come to rescue him, the young Union lieutenant was momentarily distracted.

General Lyon took advantage of the confusion and drew his pistols from under the pillow and shot the young Pennsylvanian through the head, dropping him dead where he stood.

Then Lyon and his quartermaster made as much noise as possible and darted out the front door and fired several shots into the party surrounding the house. At that point, Lyon and his man abruptly changed directions and ran out the back door, firing at the same time, and running for the mountains in the area.

As Lyon tells it, "For the first two hundred yards from the house, the federal soldiers were within twenty steps of me, crying, 'Here he goes, shoot him.'"

At that point, Lyon, still fleeing the oncoming soldiers, happened upon a creek too deep to wade across. He grabbed a log and made his way to an island, where he grabbed another log and swam furiously to the opposite shore.

Hearing voices, Lyon plunged himself down into the cold water before realizing that the voices he heard were his own men.

Lyon finishes the story: "After the excitement which I had undergone had somewhat subsided, I found myself without a hat or coat and with only one sock on, all my horses, three in number, having been captured by the enemy."

But by the middle of March of 1865, Lyon was without men, who had deserted and were fighting as guerrillas in the area. By March 26th he made his way to Selma, Alabama to help his old friend Forrest.

But soon the war was over, and Lyon fled to Mexico for a year before returning to Kentucky in 1866, when he was pardoned on June 11, 1866. For a while he farmed, until being elected to the Kentucky House of Representatives from 1899 to1901, and he became an active advocate for veteran affairs.

Part of the land for the state penitentiary near Eddyville was built on Lyon's property. For a time, Lyon served on the State Penitentiary Commission.

He died on April 25, 1907 and was buried in Eddyville Cemetery.

His had been an eventful life: an orphan who had distinguished himself in service to the nation, to the Confederacy, and in the end, also, to the United States when the wounds of war began to heal.

Today, few Kentuckians have heard of Hylan Lyon, but at the height of his power, in western Kentucky in the winter of 1864 and 1865, his name seemingly was on the everyone's lips.

Kentucky's Confederate Trickster: General Adam "Stovepipe" Johnson

Not since the Trojan Horse has anybody been so full of military tricks as those displayed during the Civil War by Henderson County, Kentucky native Adam "Stovepipe" Johnson.

While he makes most books on the war's oddities for his stovepipe subterfuge, actually his ability as a Confederate trickster was tested on more than just one occasion.

According to his autobiography, General Adam Rankin Johnson was born in Henderson, Kentucky on February 8, 1834, son of a Thomas J. Johnson, a local physician and Juliet Rankin Johnson, the daughter of Dr. Adam Rankin, also a physician.

Feeling restless and in need of adventure, Johnson left Kentucky as a young man to try his luck first in Burnet County, Texas, but then later on the Texas frontier. He soon garnered a reputation as an effective and brave Indian fighter as well as a top-notch surveyor, for many times surveying such territory demanded just as much skill with a rifle as a transit.

But when the Civil War broke out, Rankin hurried back to Kentucky to seek even more excitement and to fight on the side of the South.

He quickly located General Nathan Bedford Forrest and served him as an able and valuable scout, deftly escaping with Forrest and his men from Fort Donelson under siege from General Ulysses S. Grant's troops.

While Johnson enjoyed his days with Forrest, Forrest sensed that Johnson would be happier freelancing as a Partisan Ranger than he would as being the eyes and ears of Forrest's regiment.

Although authorized by the Confederate Congress, Partisan Rangers operated much like guerrillas, except that they followed orders given by Confederate commanders. John Singleton Mosby's Rangers patrolling their rural area of Virginia are good examples of both the effectiveness and stealth of groups like them. So when fellow Kentuckian General John C. Breckinridge requested his services as a Ranger, Johnson jumped at the chance.

Breckinridge quickly realized the talents of Johnson and sent him on several missions behind enemy lines. Soon after the Battle of Shiloh, Breckinridge told Johnson that he had a job for him.

After the Battle of Farmington, Tennessee on October 7, 1863, and accompanied by Colonel Robert M. Martin, a frequent companion of Johnson's, who was just as full of tricks as Johnson himself, the two Rebels were given the job of observing the movement of the Federals from a road behind the Yankee lines.

Unfortunately, the one spot that afforded the best view was not the easiest spot to reach since it was a clump of brush in an open field. But concealment was only part of the problem; reaching the stand of bushes was the real task. Several Rebel soldiers had already been sacrificed in quest of the information Breckinridge sought.

Carefully and slowly, Johnson and Martin crawled across the field, shielded only by a slight ravine, Johnson moving from one direction, Martin the other.

Martin soon realized that Johnson would likely attract enemy fire at any moment, so Martin, using brush, quickly constructed two dummies that would serve to draw enemy fire away from Johnson while he sneaked into his observation point.

The trick worked.

Soon the Union troops poured round after round into Martin's dummies, which he had concealed just enough to invite enemy fire, while he stole away to meet Johnson, who had by this time made it to his observation point.

But Johnson, realizing that the brushy thicket was not thick enough to hide both of them safely, then turned to a trick he had used many times fighting Indians.

Johnson recounts the rest: "Once in the thicket, about one hundred yards from the Union sharpshooters, we were comparatively safe, but I made our place of refuge impervious to Federal eyes by cutting and sticking bushes up to make a screen." The hastily built screen worked.

Mission accomplished: Breckinridge had his information.

Breckinridge's next mission for Johnson and Martin promised to be an even more important one.

The pair were to use a secret cipher to identify themselves when they arrived in Henderson, Kentucky, where they were to flank the Yankees and, in Breckinridge's words, "bring out all the Kentuckians you can to serve as Southern soldiers." But Breckinridge gave Johnson and Martin an added incentive: "If you bring out enough men, you shall have the command of them."

Johnson now had a chance to command his own group of Southern soldiers–and he was going to make the most of it.

On the way, Johnson and Martin separated for a time, while Johnson stopped at a farmhouse for supper and to feed his horses at the home of a Rebel sympathizer, who had just returned after having lost an arm at the Battle of Shiloh.

But the Johnny Reb had one more ailment that would ironically prove to actually be a stroke of good luck for Johnson: the poor soldier had a horrible case of poison oak that his wife was gently treating with some kind of poultice.

Soon the sound of horses interrupted the cool of the evening. It was the Federals—and they quickly surrounded the house.

As Johnson records: "I was much alarmed at being caught there in a trap, but a happy thought struck me...."

Not dressed in a uniform, but suspiciously associated with a known Confederate soldier, Johnson quickly and punctiliously asked for the Federals' surgeon.

The major in the command quipped, "What in the world do you want with a surgeon?"

Johnson shot back: "Why, we have a sick Confederate soldier in the house and we are afraid that he has smallpox."

The major replied, "The thunder you say!" and sent the surgeon in to examine the man of the house.

Johnson quickly sneaked back into the house and instructed the afflicted soldier to "moan and groan and say that his bones were breaking with fever."

After a very quick examination, the doctor "pronounced it an undoubted case of smallpox in its worst form."

As the Yankees rode off, Johnson heard the Union major say to one of his men: "I would take that fellow along to show us the way if he had not been so exposed to that case of smallpox."

Johnson chuckled to himself.

His hometown of Henderson was the scene for his next ruse. He had learned that a large number of Union soldiers occupied a brick house in the city: a temptation he could not resist. So Johnson, Martin, and another Ranger named Frank Owen stole into town one dark night and hid behind a plank fence, out of sight of two sentinels, marching back and forth in front of the house on guard duty. As Johnson and his companions crouched down behind the fence, a Captain Daily and a Lieutenant Lyon were, in Johnson's colorful words, "walking up and down the pavement, unconsciously tempting the marksmanship of their antagonists...."

Adam "Stovepipe" Johnson: Kentucky's Confederate trickster. Courtesy of the Kentucky Historical Society.

The plan the three Rangers hatched was to have Johnson take out the two officers with his shotgun, while Martin and Owen would shoot the two sentinels.

The moment came. Johnson blasted away, and Martin and Owen quickly followed with five loud bursts of fire.

The Yankees hastily grabbed their wounded, ducked inside, and barricaded the doors behind them.

Johnson, Martin, and Owen quickly reloaded and circled around to the building's back door where they found one lone Yankee that they loaded with bullets as he scurried into the house, snapped, and bolted the door.

Confused, the Union men fired blindly out windows at an enemy that was not there. Blasting away, the Yankees shot anything that moved, including a poor old sow roaming the streets at night.

The blood that the hog left in the street was to the Yankees the next morning an irrefutable sign that one of their many attackers had been wounded.

Imagine Johnson's satisfaction when the next day the *Evansville*

Journal in wild headlines read: "Bloody War on the Border, Provost Guard Attacked by Three Hundred Guerillas! After a Desperate Resistance of over Nine Hours They Succeed in Driving the Enemy off with Heavy Loss!"

There was no word on the poor sow.

But, of course, the most famous ruse Johnson is associated with is also the trick that will forever identify him as not just General Adam R. Johnson, but as General "Stovepipe Johnson."

His description of what happened is a study in understatement and modesty.

According to Johnson, a Union arsenal housed hundreds of guns just across the river from Henderson in the little town of Newburgh, Indiana, upstream from Evansville and near where the Green River merges with the Ohio.

To Johnson's mind the South could use all those guns, so he and twenty-seven men planned to attack the brick house where the guns were stored and "rescue" the weapons for the Confederacy.

The plan was simple: Johnson, Felix Akin, and Frank Owen would slide across the river in a skiff and take possession of the arsenal, while Martin and the rest of the men would follow and fight their way to the building in support of Johnson, Akin, and Owen. Martin and his men would then transport the guns across the river.

As part of the plan, Johnson ordered that the men's horses be left in prominent view on the Kentucky side of the river.

The next order was a stroke of genius: Johnson told his men to take two pairs of old wagon wheels and their axles to fashion what appeared to be two cannon; only instead of two cannon, Johnson's men mounted a charred log on one and a length of stovepipe on the other.

Back in Newburgh, to their surprise, Johnson and his two other men found the doors of the arsenal standing wide open. Johnson surveyed the situation and promptly bolted the doors and barricaded the three of them inside.

Seeing several unarmed Newburgh residents outside, Johnson sought to deal with the situation before the men could put up a stiff fight. He trailed the men into a local hotel where he found to his surprise about eighty Yankee soldiers with guns cocked and ready to fire.

This called for some quick thinking.

Johnson, assuming an air of authority, told the men that if they would throw down their guns before his men arrived, the Yankee soldiers would not be harmed. Johnson did not say how many men he had, however.

The bluff worked.

The men soon stacked their arms and gave up.

But just at that moment, a Union officer, a Colonel Bethel, burst into the room and demanded to know what was going on. One of his own men blurted out that, "They have got all the streets guarded and are coming this way."

The officer quickly surrendered and submitted the company's muster roll prior to being paroled.

But the danger was not over.

According to reports, the local home guards, two hundred and fifty strong, were assembling and planning an attack.

Johnson addressed his prisoners: "Gentlemen, I hear that there is a home guard near that is about to attack me, and I must say that I came here to get these guns, I have them, and I propose to keep them; I want nothing more and do not intend to disturb any of the citizens or any of their property, but if I am hindered or fired upon, I'll shell this town to the ground!"

Turning to Colonel Bethel, he said, "I see, sir, that you have a field-glass and by looking across the river you can see that I am prepared to carrying out my threat," motioning across the river at the two "cannon," barely visible, yet no less frightening to all the Yankees.

The colonel looked at his own house and quickly concluded that it would be one of the first to be destroyed. He swiftly gave the word to turn back the advancing home guard.

Johnson crowed: "I, with my body guard of two men, walked quickly down [to the river], and pushed off into the river, unmolested...."

But as Martin and his men were loading the confiscated arms, Johnson noticed a Federal gunboat chugging up the river, heading toward his men on the Kentucky side at the mouth of the Green River. Johnson speedily dispatched his men to two positions on opposite sides of the Green River. As the gunboat steamed up the mouth of the river, Johnson's men opened fire, shouting and yelling at the top of their lungs, so scaring the captain that he was convinced that it was an enemy force three times its size. The captain impulsively reversed course, and steamed away, allowing Martin and his men to haul the arms across the river unharmed, and to fool the Yankees one more time.

There were other tricks at other times for Johnson and his Tenth Kentucky Partisan Rangers, but on October 21, 1864, on a mission at Grubb's Crossroads in Caldwell County, Kentucky, one of Johnson's own men accidentally shot him in the head, not killing him, but permanently blinding him. The general was then captured and imprisoned in Fort Warren in Boston Harbor in Massachusetts for the rest of the war.

Returning to Texas, according to *Handbook of Texas*, Johnson founded the city of Marble Falls, appropriately nicknamed "the blind man's town." Not dying until October 20, 1922, he lived a full and productive eighty-eight years as founder of Texas Mining Improvement Company and as a contractor for the Overland Mail Company. Revered by his Texas friends, he was known besides his sobriquet "Stovepipe" Johnson as simply and aptly, "The Swamp Fox of Kentucky."

About the Author

Dr. Marshall Myers was reared in rural Meade County, near Battletown. After graduating from Meade County High School in 1961, he took bachelor's and master's degrees in English at Kentucky Wesleyan College and Eastern Kentucky University. After four years of college teaching at Elizabethtown Community College and Kentucky Wesleyan, he studied for a Ph.D. in American literature and linguistics at Kansas State University, but left graduate work there because of illness. He later returned to graduate work at the University of Louisville, earning a Ph.D. in rhetoric and composition in 1994. Having taught at the middle school, secondary school and college levels, Myers is now a Professor of English at Eastern Kentucky University where he teaches undergraduate and graduate courses in linguistics and rhetoric.

Myers has authored more than two hundred articles, poems, academic pieces, and short stories, as well as three books: *On the Inside*, a collection of poems; *Real Toads*, a chapbook of poems on a single theme; and *Barefoot*, a collection of short stories. His articles and reviews on the Civil War have appeared in *Kentucky Explorer, The Kentucky Civil War Journal*, and *The Register of the Kentucky Historical Society*. He serves as president of the Madison County Civil War Roundtable and contributes a bi-monthly column on the Civil War in Kentucky to the organization's newsletter. He is married to Dr. Lynn Gillaspie, also a member of the faculty at E.K.U. He has two daughters, Mitzi Gacki and Marti Brown; five grandsons and one great grandson. He is the son of the late Carol Clement of Brandenburg and Clarice Myers of Battletown.

Index

A

Abbott, Richard 187
Abell, Betsy 40, 43
Adair, John 194
Adair, Kate 194
Ainsworth, F.C. 171
Akin, Felix 215
Albany, Kentucky 105, 122
Aleman, Jesse 173
Alexandria, Tennessee 195
Alger, Horatio 17
Anderson River 27
Andersonville, Georgia 145
Athertonville, Kentucky 22
Atlanta, Georgia 163, 205

B

Bacon, Colonel 177
Bacon Creek 195
Baker, Clauscine R. 203, 204
Baker, Jean 82
Ball's Bluff 174
Bardstown, Kentucky 39, 71, 106, 125, 195
Barkley, Alben 57
Barton, William 29, 31
Bassham, Ben 163
Baton Rouge, Louisiana 74, 163
Battle of Antietam 172
Battle of Buena Vista 84, 194
Battle of Chickamauga 76, 77, 78, 100
Battle of Cynthiana 91
Battle of Gettysburg 36, 80, 153, 172
Battle of Green River 177
Battle of Manassas 80
Battle of Middle Creek 84
Battle of Murfreesboro 116
Battle of Perryville 86, 115, 137
Battle of Richmond 100
Battle of Rowletts Station 177
Battle of Shiloh 74, 115, 163, 172, 178, 189, 194, 195, 212, 213
Battle of Stones River 116
Battle of Tippecanoe 47
Battle of Woodsonville 177
Beard, Bob 164
Beatty, Tinker Dave 199
Beecher, Henry Ward 142
Bell, J.F. 63
Bell, Mary 172
Bell, Molly 172
Bethel, Colonel 216
Billingsley, Captain 177
Bissell, Alfred 188, 189
Black Hawk War 83
Blair, Montgomery 54
Blanton, DeAnne 171
Blue River Island 122, 124, 126
Bonaparte, Napoleon 133
Booth, John Wilkes 179, 183
Boston Harbor, Massachusetts 217
Boston, Massachusetts 190
Botts, John Minor 92
Bowling Green, Kentucky 164, 177, 194
Boyle, Jeremiah T. 52, 97, 195, 197
Bragg, Braxton 75, 79, 86, 87, 90, 104, 113, 114, 115, 116, 117, 118, 119, 121
Bramlette, Thomas 52, 100, 142
Brandenburg, Kentucky 107, 121, 139, 197
Breckinridge, John Cabell 50, 74, 75, 76, 92, 111, 114, 115, 116, 117, 118, 119, 212, 213
Breckinridge, Robert 139
Brice Cross Roads, Mississippi 205, 206
Briggs, Ernestine 20
Briggs, Harold 20
Brooklyn, New York 53
Brown, Dee Alexander 95
Brown, E.O. 159
Brown, John C. 173
Brown, Joseph B. 159
Browning, Orville 42
Bruce, Horatio W. 72
Buchanan, James 64, 114
Buckner, Richard 140
Buckner, Simon Bolivar 73, 115, 180, 194
Buell, Don Carlos 74, 177
Buffington Island, Ohio 108
Buford, Harry T. 104, 172, 173, 174, 175, 176, 177, 178
Bull Run 80, 174
Burbridge, Stephen Gano 52, 53, 81, 160, 199, 200, 201
Burke, Curtis R. 147, 148
Burkesville, Kentucky 105, 106, 196, 207
Burlingame, Michael 35
Burns, Mary 172
Burns, Robert 33
Burnside, Ambrose 196, 197, 198
Bush, Isaac 18
Butler, Benjamin 62

C

Cadiz, Kentucky 207
Calhoun, John C. 57
Cameron, Salmon P. 174
Cameron, Simon 194
Campbellsville, Kentucky 106, 195, 207
Camp Douglas 146, 147, 148, 149
Camp Hobson 194
Camp Nelson 187, 190
Cannelton Dam 122, 124
Cannelton, Indiana 157

220

Capitol Rotunda 163
Carlisle, Pennsylvania 71
Carter, Jimmy 158
Carthage, Tennessee 196
Castleman, John 131
Catton, Bruce 113
Champion Hill, Kentucky 205
Chapman, Conrad Wise 116, 163, 164, 165, 166
Chapman, John Gadsby 163
Charleston, South Carolina 109
Chattanooga, Tennessee 75, 80, 118, 195
Chenault, David Waller 101, 104, 105, 106
Chicago, Illinois 130, 131, 146
Chickamauga Creek 75
Chickamauga, Georgia 163
Cincinnati, Ohio 47, 52, 108
Civil War 9, 11, 12, 13, 24, 49, 54, 63, 64, 66, 71, 75, 77, 82, 83, 87, 90, 101, 109, 111, 113, 121, 127, 132, 133, 135, 138, 139, 145, 146, 151, 157, 162, 163, 165, 169, 171, 172, 174, 179, 185, 187, 201, 202, 204, 211
Clalin, Frances 172
Clark, Thomas 137, 138, 164
Clarke, Jerome 89
Clarke, Marcellus Jerome 99
Clay, Cassius 84
Clay, Henry 57, 58, 59, 60, 61, 62, 64, 72, 194
Clay, John 62
Cleburne, Patrick 117
Cleveland, Ohio 201
Clinton, Illinois 189, 192
Clinton, William Jefferson 191
Cloverport, Kentucky 25
Cluke, Roy 99
Cofer, Martin H. 72
Coffeeville, Kentucky 205
Collins, Sara 172
Columbia, Kentucky 106, 196
Columbus, Kentucky 175, 176
Columbus, Ohio 108, 128, 131, 198
Cooper, John Sherman 57
Cooper, William Jr. 140
Coopersmith, Andrew 151
Corby, William 153
Corinth, Mississippi 74
Corydon, Indiana 197
Crawford, Josiah 17
Crimean War 90
Crittenden, George 69, 139

Crittenden, John Jordan 57, 63, 64, 65, 66, 67, 68, 69
Crittenden, Thomas L. 69, 139, 194
Crockett, Davy 17
Crump, W.D. 148
Cumberland River 188, 189, 196, 203, 204
Cynthiana, Kentucky 200

D

Dahlgren, John 129
Dahlgren, Ulric 129
Daily, Captain 214
Danville, Kentucky 100
Davidson, Catherine E. 172
Davis, Jefferson 12, 51, 63, 65, 67, 73, 74, 81, 84, 87, 115, 118, 119, 129, 130, 131, 177, 180, 181, 182, 183
Davis, J.M. 152
Davis, Lois 152
Davis, William C. 84, 87, 118, 167
Derby, Indiana 122
Dill, John T. 28, 29
Dill, Lin 28, 29
Donald, David Herbert 36
Douglas, Stephen A. 65, 146, 186
Douglass, Frederick 185
Dowdey, Clifford 113
Dracut, Massachusetts 152
Dry Tortugus 93
Duke, Basil 89, 90, 97, 99, 123, 125, 154, 155, 198

E

Early, Jubal 172
Eddyville, Kentucky 192, 206, 207, 209
Edmonds, Sara Emma 172
Elizabethtown, Kentucky 18, 22, 25, 71, 73, 103, 125, 195, 197, 207
Ellsworth, George "Lightning" 89, 90, 91, 95, 96, 97, 99
Elmira, New York 145
Evansville, Indiana 215

F

Farmington, Tennessee 212
Farragut, Admiral David G. 152
Ferguson, Champ 53, 89, 99, 199
Fife, Joel A. 148
Fillmore, Millard 63

Fisher, Walter R. 67, 68
Folly Island, South Carolina 190
Ford's Theatre 179
Forrest, Nathan Bedford 204, 205, 206, 209, 211
Fort Donelson 178, 180, 189, 204, 211
Fort Henry 189
Fort Lincoln, Texas 71
Fort Myers, Florida 203
Fort Sumter 194
Fort Warren 204, 217
Fort Yuma, California 203
Foster, J.G. 110
Fowler, Wiley P. 52
Frankfort, Kentucky 47, 72, 83, 96, 97
Franklin, Benjamin 17

G

Garfield, James A. 84, 85, 86, 179
Garnettsville, Kentucky 107, 197
Garrard, Kenner 158
Gentryville, Indiana 25
Georgetown, Kentucky 97
Gettysburg, Pennsylvania 121
Gillaspie, Lynn 9
Glover, John M. 173
Gollaher, Austin 21
Goodridge, Ellen 172
Gordon, John B. 116
Grahamville, South Carolina 190
Grand Rivers, Kentucky 192
Grant, Ulysses S. 55, 74, 79, 109, 115, 180, 189, 201, 205, 211
Graves, Nelly 172
Green, Johnny 168
Green, Mrs. Bowling 41
Green River 104, 106, 177, 178, 195, 215, 216
Greensburg, Kentucky 193, 194, 198
Gregory, Eli S. 31
Grenfell, George St. Leger 89, 90, 91, 92, 93, 99
Griffith, Paddy 83
Grove, Clary 17
Grubb's Crossroads 217
Guerrant, Edward O. 84, 87
Gulliver, John P. 23

H

Halleck, Henry 201
Hamilton, Alexander 59

Hammond, J.H. 160
Hanchett, William 182
Hanks, Dennis 20
Hanks, James 20
Hanks, Lucey Shipley 20
Hardee, William Joseph 75, 117, 177
Harding, Aaron 188
Hardin, Lucinda Barbour 71
Hardinsburg, Kentucky 25
Harrisburg, Pennsylvania 159
Harris, Ira 80, 81
Harrison, Lowell 9, 13, 50, 51, 54, 114, 116, 139
Harrison, William Henry 47, 63
Hartford, Kentucky 207
Hartsville, Tennessee 103
Hatch, John P. 190
Havana, Cuba 173
Hawes, Richard 101
Hay, John 62
Hay, Melba Porter 59
Haycraft, Samuel 19
Hayes, Charles 9
Hazel, Caleb 23
Helm, Ben Hardin 71, 72, 73, 74, 75, 76, 77
Helm, Emilie Todd 72, 77, 78, 79, 80, 81, 82
Helm, John LaRue 71
Helm, Katherine 77, 81
Hemphill, John 67
Henderson, Kentucky 38, 211, 213, 214, 215
Henry, David 53
Henry, Margaret 172
Henry, W.D. 148
Herndon, William 20, 24, 39, 43
Hesseltine, William 146
Hickman, Kentucky 175
Hill, D.H. 76
Hines, Thomas Henry 89, 93, 99, 107, 121, 122, 123, 124, 125, 126, 127, 128, 129, 130, 131, 132
Hobson, Edward 107, 193, 194, 195, 196, 197, 198, 199, 200, 201, 202
Hobson, Lucy Kirtley 193
Hobson, William 193
Hodgenville, Kentucky 18, 19, 49, 73
Hodges, Jennie 172
Hoffert, Sylvia D. 172, 178
Hoffman, William 146
Holland, J.G. 23
Holt, Joseph 84
Honey Hill 191
Hood, John Bell 134, 207

Hopkinsville, Kentucky 139, 207
Horse Cave, Kentucky 96
Howard, Frances Thomas 161
Howell, Carl 21, 23
Hubbell, John T. 186, 187
Hughes, Susan Lyons 135, 137

I

Indianapolis, Indiana 157
Iverson, Alfred 65

J

Jackman, John S. 167, 168
Jackson, John 76
Jackson, Mississippi 75, 173
Jackson, T.J. "Stonewall" 151
Jacob, Richard Taylor 52
Joan of Arc 174
Johnson, Adam Rankin "Stovepipe" 99, 199, 206, 211, 212, 213, 214, 215, 216, 217
Johnson, Andrew 158
Johnson, E. Polk 53
Johnson Island, Ohio 108, 204
Johnson, Juliet Rankin 211
Johnson, Thomas J. 211
Johnson, William Preston 181
Johnston, Albert Sidney 74, 127, 158
Johnston, Andrew 36
Johnston, Joseph E. 75, 119
Jones, Edgar DeWitt 58
Jones, Martha 54
Jones, Mary Joseph 207
Jones, Stephen 160
Jones, Terry 205
Jones, Willis F. 54, 55
Judah, Henry M. 107, 196, 198

K

Kellar's Bridge 200
Kennedy, John F. 57, 179
Kingston, Kentucky 101
Kirwan, Albert D. 66, 68, 168
Klotter, James 9, 12, 114, 139
Knob Creek Farm 17, 19, 21, 25
Knoxville, Tennessee 115

L

La Grange, Kentucky 122, 127, 203

Lake Michigan 146
Lebanon Junction, Kentucky 195
Lebanon, Kentucky 97, 106, 195, 196
Lebanon, Tennessee 100, 102
Lecomte, Joe 84
Ledbetter, Patsy S. 64
Lee, Robert E. 36, 73, 90, 91, 121, 134, 151, 158
Levy, George 145, 146, 149
Lewisport, Kentucky 27, 31
Lexington, Kentucky 79, 82, 95, 96, 97, 127, 135, 140, 195
Libby Prison 129
Licking River 200
Lincoln, Abraham 12, 13, 17, 18, 19, 20, 21, 22, 23, 24, 25, 27, 28, 29, 30, 33, 34, 35, 36, 37, 38, 39, 40, 41, 42, 43, 45, 46, 47, 48, 49, 50, 51, 52, 53, 54, 55, 57, 58, 59, 60, 62, 63, 64, 65, 66, 67, 71, 72, 73, 76, 78, 79, 80, 81, 82, 83, 84, 93, 114, 122, 123, 129, 130, 146, 152, 160, 174, 179, 180, 181, 182, 183, 186
Lincoln, Mary Todd 24, 37, 45, 49, 72, 77, 78, 79, 80, 82
Lincoln, Nancy Hanks 18, 20, 73
Lincoln, Robert 80
Lincoln, Sarah 18, 23
Lincoln, Tad 81
Lincoln, Thomas 18, 20, 21, 22, 25, 45
Lincoln, Willie 79, 80
Logan, Stephen T. 24
Louisville, Kentucky 22, 46, 53, 72, 83, 106, 107, 157, 158, 159, 162, 173, 180, 182, 194, 196, 197, 198
Lyon, Elizabeth Martin 203
Lyon, Hylan Benton 203, 204, 205, 206, 207, 208, 209, 214
Lyon, Matthew Jr. 203

M

Madisonville, Kentucky 207
Marble Falls, Texas 217
Marietta, Georgia 158, 159
Marrowbone, Kentucky 196
Marshall, Humphrey 83, 84, 85, 86, 87
Marshall, John 47
Marshall, Samuel D. 47

Martin, Robert M. 212, 213, 214, 215, 216, 217
Masters, Edgar Lee 39
Matthews, William 9
McClellan, George 49, 160
McCook, Alexander McD. 177
McCreary, Edmund R. 100, 106, 107, 108, 109, 110, 111
McCreary, James Bennett 100, 101, 102, 103, 104, 105, 111
McCreary, Sabrina Bennett 100
McDonald, Rose 161, 162
McDowell, Samuel 139
McKinley, William 179
McMinnville, Tennessee 102
McMurtry, R. Gerald 71, 72, 73, 74, 76
McRae, Bennie J. 190
McWhiney, Gerald 113
McWhiney, Grady 87
Meeker, Caroline 24, 29, 30, 31, 37, 45
Melnick, John 152, 153
Mendenhall, John 117
Mexican War 84, 180
Middle Creek, Kentucky 11
Midway, Kentucky 96
Mill Springs, Kentucky 11
Missionary Ridge 163
Mississippi River 175
Mitchell, Joseph B. 113, 205
Montgomery, Alabama 73
Monticello, Kentucky 105
Moore, Absalom 103
Morganfield, Kentucky 47
Morgan, Henrietta 140, 141
Morgan, John Hunt 12, 89, 90, 91, 92, 93, 95, 96, 97, 99, 102, 103, 104, 106, 107, 108, 115, 121, 122, 123, 125, 127, 128, 137, 140, 143, 154, 193, 195, 196, 197, 198, 199, 200, 201
Morocco, India 90
Morris Island 110
Morse, Flo 138
Morton, Oliver 123
Mosby, John Singleton 212
Mudd, Samuel 93
Muldraugh's Hill 103
Mundy, Sue 199
Munfordville, Kentucky 177, 195, 196, 199
Murfeesboro, Tennessee 74, 102
Murray, J. Ogden 110
Myers, Carol Cushman 9

Myers, Clarice Jr. 9
Myers, Marshall 9

N

Nashville, Tennessee 22, 103, 159, 207
Nation, J.B. 180
Neal, Julia 137
Nelson, William "Bull" 51
Newberne, North Carolina 190
Newburgh, Indiana 99, 215
New Lisbon, Ohio 198
Newman, Price 169
Newmarket, Kentucky 106
New Orleans, Louisiana 173, 174, 190
New Salem, Kentucky 39, 40, 45
Noe, Kenneth 101
Nolin Creek 18
Nolin Station 207
Nutgrass, Albert 193, 194, 195, 198, 200, 201, 202

O

Obie River 105
Ohio River 27, 28, 47, 50, 52, 107, 108, 121, 122, 123, 124, 157, 175, 189, 197, 215
Old Cumberland Road 21
Ottawa, Illinois 58
Overland Mail Company 217
Owen, Frank 214, 215
Owens, Mary 24, 39, 40, 41, 42, 43
Owens, Nancy Grayham 39
Owens, Nathaniel 39

P

Paducah, Kentucky 143, 175
Paine, Eleazor Arthur 52
Palmer, John M. 52, 160
Pate, Arretta 30
Pate, Samuel 28, 29, 31, 45
Pearl River 168
Pensacola, Florida 174
Perryville, Kentucky 11, 12, 101, 104
Peter, Frances 140, 141
Peyton, Samuel O. 207
Phelps, Edward 161
Philadelphia, Pennsylvania 17
Phillips, Inan 105
Pigeon Creek 45
Pittsburg Landing 194
Pleasant Hill 135, 137, 138

Polk, Leonidas 75, 175, 176, 177
Pollard, Alabama 75
Potomac River 181
Pound Gap, Kentucky 85
Powell, Lazarus 64
Prentice, George 139, 159
Preston, William 84
Princeton, Kentucky 203, 207

Q

Qualshm, Indian Chief 204

R

Ramage, James 92, 132
Rankin, Adam 211
Rankin, Aminda Rogers 21
Ray, Dan 154, 156
Readville, Massachusetts 190
Red Hill, Alabama 208
Remington, Ida 172
Richmond, Kentucky 9, 11, 54, 85, 86, 93, 100, 101, 104, 111, 133, 141, 152, 173, 180, 182, 206
Riddle, George W. 47
Riney, Zachariah 22
Robb, J.S. 134
Robertson, James L. 145
Rock Island, Illinois 130, 131
Rome, Indiana 122
Rosecrans, William S. 75, 103
Rose, Jerlene 9
Rosencrantz, Otto F. 164, 165
Roswell, Georgia 158
Rutledge, Ann 24, 38, 39

S

Sanders, S.W. 204, 205, 206
Sandusky, Ohio 108
Sangamon River 60
Schofield, J.M. 160
Schultz, Duane 127, 128, 129, 131
Scott, Walter 90
Selma, Alabama 79, 209
Seward, William 27, 64, 65
Shackleford 198
Shackleford, James 196
Shakespeare, William 33
Shawneetown, Illinois 47
Shelby, Isaac 63
Shelbyville, Kentucky 125
Sherman, William Tecumseh 158, 159, 160, 162, 189, 199, 205
Shinseki, Eric K. 191
Sickles, Dan 80

Simpson, George B. 47
Sinking Springs Farm 18, 21
Skinner, Fred H. 203
Smith, Andrew Jackson 185, 188, 191, 192
Smith, Elijah 188, 189, 190
Smith, John David 140
Smith, Kirby 143
Smithland, Kentucky 192
Smithville, Tennessee 195
Somerset, Kentucky 97, 105
Sparrow, Henry 20
Sparta, Tennessee 91, 102, 196
Speed, Joshua 24, 46, 54
Springfield, Illinois 33, 72, 78
Springfield, Kentucky 103, 106, 195
Stanton, Edwin M. 157
Stapleton, Kentucky 125
Starr, Stephen Z. 127
Stephens, Alexander H. 173
Stephensport, Kentucky 122
Stone's River 118, 163
Stuart, J.E.B. 92
Stuart, John T. 24
Swentor, Meredith 84, 87
Swiggett, Howard 95, 96

T

Taylor, Hancock 180
Taylor, Joseph Pannell 180
Taylor, Sarah Knox 180
Taylorsville, Kentucky 125
Taylor, Walker 179, 180, 181, 182, 183
Taylor, Zachary 180
Tebbs Bend 196
Tebbs Bend, Kentucky 195
Terry, Benjamin 177
Texas Mining Improvement Company 217
Thomas, Benjamin 68
Thomas, George H. 75
Thomas, Lorenzo 187
Thompson, John 131
Thrasher, Caroline 31
Thrasher, Eli 30, 31
Tidwell, William A. 182
Todd, Betsy 79
Todd, Robert 72
Tompkinsville, Kentucky 91, 195, 196
Toombs, Robert 65
Townsend, William H. 50, 55
Troy, Indiana 27
Tullahoma, Tennessee 104
Tyler, John 63

V

Varhola, Michael J. 133, 134
Velazquez, Loreta Janeta 171, 172, 173, 174, 176, 178
Versailles, Kentucky 54, 63
Vicksburg, Kentucky 205
Vineyard, Jesse 43
Viney Grove, Kentucky 25
Virginia, Brookneal 20
Virginia, Fort Monroe 79
Virginia, Princeton West 86
Virginia, Richmond 51, 87, 129
Virginia, Saltville 199

W

Walker, Dale L. 161
Walker, Mary Edwards 157, 158, 159, 160, 161, 162
Warner, John 189
War of 1812 59, 63, 193
Warren, Louis A. 20, 22, 47
Washington, D.C. 51, 95, 119, 131, 159, 163, 173, 180, 181, 201
Washington, George 17, 50
Waters, Peggy 18
Watson, Ensign James 197
Webster, Daniel 57
Weems, Parson 17
West Point, Ohio 126
White, Charles 153
White House, The 45, 54, 77, 79, 80, 81, 82, 180
Wildcat Mountain, Kentucky 11
Wilder, Burt G. 191
Willcox, Orlando 123
Williams, Alice 173
Williams, T. Harry 113
Willich, August 177
Wilson, Fanny 76, 172
Wirz, Henry 145
Wise, Mary 172
Wolford, Frank Lane 196, 198
Woodward, Isaiah 66
Wright, Mary 172
Wynne, Parson 154, 155, 156
Wythe, George 59

Y

Young, Bennett 206